THE STRENGTH TO STRIVE

by
David Pease

with foreword by
Dr. William Larkin, Ph.D.

LIFETIME BOOKS, INC.
Hollywood, Florida

This publication is designed to provide accurate and authoritative information in regard to the subject matter covered. It is sold with the understanding that the publisher is not engaged in rendering legal, accounting, or other professional service. If legal advice or other assistance is required, the services of a competent professional person should be sought. *From a Declaration of Principles jointly adopted by a Committee of the American Bar Association and a Committee of Publishers.*

Library of Congress Cataloging-in-Publication Data

Pease, David (David R.)
    The strength to strive / by David Pease.
        p.   cm.
    ISBN 0-8119-0770-8
    1. Success--Psychological aspects.   I. Title.
    H.   II. Title
    BF637.S8P424   1992
    158'.1--dc20

                                                92-38388
                                                CIP

Manufactured in the United States of America

1 2 3 4 5 6 7 8 9 0

DEDICATION

To Dave, Casey and Brian

May this book inspire you and countless others to redefine what's possible in your life; to experience first hand the power of belief, the will to prepare and the propulsion to begin and to persevere...all component and defining attributes of the "strength to strive."

TABLE OF CONTENTS

PART I
The Strength to Strive

PART II
The Me Encounter

Section 1
The M.E. (Me Encounter) Weekend

Section 2
Returning Home

FOREWORD

David Pease's *The Strength to Strive* and *The M.E. Weekend* are simple and straightforward contributions to the wide assortment of self-empowerment materials that are available today. What impresses me most is that the process of self-discovery he encourages, asks the participant to think through what he or she really wants. The various exercises designed to help the reader come to grips with one's personal aim are easy and low-key. The reader is not put through pages of non-essential information, but gets going in the process very quickly. Rather than a program about how to get what you want, Pease encourages the reader to do what is absent from most empowerment material; take the time to find out what you really want, as he writes, "listen to the inner meter." Many folks today, when asked what their goals will provide for them, give answers that achieving their goals will most likely never satisfy.

Pease's techniques of keeping the participant in touch with written aims and goals, in terms of what one wants to *be*, is an essential part of this material. He is sensitive to the way in which the events of everyday life lap away at consciousness until we end up only reacting to life. His simple and easy ways of enabling people to remember where they are going is not just good material, it is essential in a world so filled with the ideas of others and the images of television. This is a good way to get in touch with, to carry, and to remember to act on one's own internal image.

For the many people today who do not want to wade through the newest fad in self-help pop psychology, this is a truthful and sincere approach to doing the kind of thinking and planning most people today don't take the time to do. One of these days, psychology and psychotherapy is going to wake up to what David Pease's intuition is causing him to write; we are tired of trudging around in problems and it is time to get on with living life. I would not hesitate to give this material to many of my clients as a useful tool for getting them to reflect on the more important concerns in their lives and to provide a bit of a motivational and inspirational source for doing so.

— Dr. William Larkin, Ph.D.
The Pastoral Theological Institute

PART I

THE STRENGTH TO STRIVE

PREFACE

THE STORY OF THE PLAQUE

ABC Sports would have described it as snatching victory from the jaws of defeat.

My thirteen-year-old son Casey, had he been born at the time, would have dismissed it simply as just another example of our Irish luck.

Perhaps.

But I believe a more powerful force was operating that day. A force that is latent in each and everyone of us. We differ only in the extent to which we learn to access it and let its power and energy flow into our lives.

My first exposure to it was unexpected, random, and couldn't have been better timed. For me, the catalyst came in the form of a plaque on a wall.

The plaque read:
> Everyday legions of men go to their graves who, for want of courage and conviction, never achieved in life what might have been theirs had they jumped into the arena and not clung to the safe and familiar.

How fortuitous to be standing before that plaque at that moment in my life.

It was an overcast, blustery day in Miami. The Christmas decorations were up and the city was alive with anticipation. But Christmas was not the focus. From the moment I landed at the

3

airport the topic on everyone's lips was football. The Miami Dolphins under new coach Don Shula were marching toward the playoffs and a city-wide love affair was in full swing.

It was late November of 1971 and I was in town for a job interview. At the age of twenty-seven, with my Army and schooling over, I was in pursuit of a dream. Just getting this far seemed a little unreal. The buzz of the city made it that much more dreamlike.

When I arrived at the address provided, the Miami Dolphin logo in the reception area and the adjacent ticket office were ample evidence mine was not the usual job search.

I was a few minutes early and the reality of actually being here at team headquarters, at the epicenter of the subject of the city's love affair, was strangely jolting. I was caught off guard by the intensity of the feelings that followed.

Here I was inches away from my goal, but something was wrong. I was starting to be pulled down by an undertow of negative thoughts.

After a lively introductory hour with Joe Robbie, Dolphin owner and Managing General Partner, I had been asked to step across the hall to Coach Shula's empty office. Mr. Robbie had another meeting and would be ready to reconvene in thirty minutes.

I was prepared for all manner of questions and contingencies except for this unexpected, thirty-minute time out. In hindsight, it was a confrontation that had been brewing for years.

At the seemingly enlightened age of twenty-seven, I was having a long-delayed showdown with the most knowledgeable, influential and elusive force in my life...myself. The question could no longer be ducked. Was I as good and as capable as my resume and cover letter claimed?

Without warning, I began the inquisition. The issue had popped into my consciousness like an uninvited guest, there was no avoiding it. I couldn't go for a run, wash the car, get a haircut, play tennis or any of the other often-invoked escapes that had kept the unpleasant issue from boiling over in the past.

It was the voice of self-doubt and it was a voice I had encountered before. It always seemed to come at inopportune times; key moments in childhood athletic contests and at various social engagements as an adolescent. But this was the worst invasion of my consciousness to date and I was beginning to self-destruct.

Even my watch had turned against me. In ten minutes I was to regroup with Mr. Robbie. Instead of pumping myself up, I was busy shooting myself in both feet.

As I turned from the window looking out over Miami's Biscayne Bay, a plaque on the far wall caught my attention. My eyes began to read but my thoughts were still swirling with the palm trees in the park across the street.

I'm not certain of the exact flow of the next few minutes, but I will be forever grateful for that plaque. It was as if fate tossed me a life ring and kept me from drowning in a self-manufactured sea of debilitating negative thoughts. I had always been a competitive sort and that plaque hit me like a bucket of cold water. The second one in as many months.

I was in a state of heightened alertness, riveted to the floor. As I contemplated the plaque's powerful message, I drew energy from its underlying sadness. I was determined not to be one of the legions who would lean back when they should have leaned in.

It was as if I had been standing in the middle of an emotional mine field and the plaque provided both the impetus and the path to safety. As my thoughts, mood and energy returned to the positive zone, I could feel my confidence level surging back. I was elated. In less than five minutes I would have an opportunity to act on this newly found determination and purpose. What a roller-coaster ride.

Something else happened during that thirty-minute lifetime. In the course of being transformed by the plaque's well-timed message and as I considered a host of less-attractive alternatives, I finally gave myself "permission" to go flat out for the job.

This is what I really wanted and had dreamed about for months. Why was I holding back?

I began to see with renewed clarity, an insight I first experienced a few months earlier in New York City. Namely, that there's a difference between doing what you really want to do in life and doing what you think you should do. I had started my working career in a large New York City bank, having listened to the "should do" voices which were very compelling. I hadn't identified a strong career direction for myself at that point, so the "should" voices had very little competition.

It's strange, as I look back on it, how a couple of seemingly random events have so influenced my life. Might this be true in your life as well?

The first directional assist came from a most unlikely source — the U. S. Army. With a freshly minted MBA, I had my eyes set on becoming a corporate lending officer in the banking community. I was not terribly excited about it, but it kept me involved and in rent money until the inevitable happened — I got drafted.

Through a fortuitous acquaintanceship at the bank, I was able to arrange a two-year assignment to the Army Athletic Association at West Point. It was during this period that I was exposed to the business side of athletics, an area I had never thought about before.

Still, the "should do" voices had a firm beachhead in my consciousness and when my two-year induction at West Point was up, I returned to banking. That's when the first bucket of cold water hit.

Banking hadn't changed much, but I sure had. I now had a frame of reference and exposure to a line of work that stirred my passions, and banking just didn't measure up in comparison.

That's when I did a very uncharacteristic thing. I resigned virtually on the spot. Perhaps it was the precipitous nature of my departure and the less-than-resounding support I felt from family and friends that contributed to the lingering doubts that I was doing the right thing. Was I a modern-day hero taking a road less traveled or had I run away from life and from responsibility?

All those thoughts and inner conflicts came flooding back as I stood staring out the window of Coach Shula's office. I was at the center of an emotional maelstrom, not doing well at all, until the plaque brought the turmoil to a quick and mood-altering resolution.

When the secretary appeared at the door and announced "Mr. Robbie is ready to see you," for the first time I was truly ready to see him.

As they say, the rest is history. I got the job, moved to Miami, got married, welcomed the first of my three sons into the world and began a journey which continues to unfold with the decision to write this book.

And to think, all because I had the good fortune or, as Casey is inclined to say, the fine Irish luck to bump into an inspirational plaque at the precise moment when I needed it the most.

In many ways, I see this book as an effort to return the favor of that plaque — to improve the odds that the next time you or a loved one need a boost or a reaffirmation, you can muster within yourself "on demand" the same positive forces that the plaque managed to pull from me, quite by chance, some twenty years ago.

To that end this book is dedicated.

INTRODUCTION

Whatever else this book is, and is ultimately judged to be, it is a book about hope, change, new beginnings and helping you regain control of your life and making it the great adventure it was meant to be.

Wherever you are in your journey, you have both the right and the capacity to be happy. It is within your reach and power to obtain and maintain the peace and contentment you seek.

The happiness we strive for is not a momentary experience such as joy. It is an ongoing attitude toward life, and how we see our life from within is the key. Becoming creatively alive in the moment, committing to pursuing a goal that's important to us, and seeding our thoughts along the way is the road map we'll be following.

We'll need three tools for the journey:
- ✓ positive self-esteem
- ✓ positive self-direction
- ✓ positive beliefs and attitudes

Our focus in the pages ahead will be largely attitudinal. Do not, however, interpret this to mean the other two tools — positive self-esteem and positive self-direction — are any less significant. The presumption is that you know where you want to go and need assistance getting started or sustaining your resolve.

Should self-esteem and self-direction be issues for you as well, you'll want to flip ahead to Chapter 7, in a moment, to see how conversant you are with your goals and beliefs. If you find the words come easily and you have a strong sense of who you are and where you want to be going, then flip back and resume reading. You can finish the balance of Chapter 7 when you come to it in normal sequence. If, however, you find you're uncertain about your goals and direction, or worse, haven't got a clue, I suggest you find a bookmark and first read Part II of this book, *The Me Encounter* — the section dealing with self-discovery and self-renewal beginning on page 119.

The intent of *The Me Encounter* is to bring you back in touch with your deepest, innermost thoughts, helping you to distinguish between what you really want to do versus what you have come to think "you should be doing." The difference is beyond night and day. Once you're in better touch with what you want to do and what your beliefs are, the program herein can provide the propulsion to bring it to fruition.

> EDITOR'S NOTE: If self-esteem and self-direction are concerns for you, please turn to Chapter 7 now to begin identifying your goals and beliefs. Depending on the ease of your answers, you may want to read *The Me Encounter* before resuming here. If self-esteem and self-direction are not issues for you, continue reading below.

◆ ◆ ◆

With your goals firmly fixed in mind, what you're about to do is create a one-minute commercial. You'll be airing this one-minute commercial to yourself at key moments of the day, beginning with the first minute each morning for a minimum of three weeks. The commercial will consist of key words and key visuals designed to invigorate you and keep you progressing towards your goal. This repetitive and focused investment, made over a twenty-one day period, will cement in place a new cornerstone of conviction and resolve that will anchor the next chapter of your life — a sturdy new foundation to support and insulate you from an unresponsive and unsupportive world, from debilitating self-doubts and negative thoughts, and from the enemies without and the enemy within. You will create a foundation that can steadfastly support your quest to regain control of your life, energy level and peace of mind.

This is one commercial you won't be zapping. On the contrary, you'll find it taking on a life of its own, slowly influencing and permeating the program that surrounds it...the program being your life.

A successful start on this new path may be only seconds away — sixty seconds to be exact — the most important minute of your life, and the subject matter of this book.

In Chapter 7 you'll begin to assemble and produce this most special of all commercials. It will be yours and yours alone; a uniquely personal creation that will inspire you for months and years to come. It will be an early dividend and a prime example of what you can create when you put your mind to it.

Like making a putt in golf, two issues need to be addressed: direction and speed. Although not a golfer, Pavlov — the noted Russian physiologist — came to this same truncated conclusion. When asked on his deathbed to what he attributed his success and success in general, he replied unflinchingly, "To passion and to gradualness." Passion has to do with direction in life. That is, involving yourself in pursuits you feel passionately about. Gradualness has to do with speed, the time you arbitrarily assign to your tasks. These two concepts — passion and gradualness — are pivotal and will arise again and again in the pages ahead. They are the philosophical underpinning of the program to come.

The central thesis of everything to follow is that much of human unhappiness is not externally caused. What we feed our minds and bodies, and the ever-present influence of early learning, continues to trigger our thoughts, our feelings, and our behavior until we decide to interrupt the cycle and choose to anchor a new, causal chain with a more life-enhancing focus.

The linchpin of the program is an uncompromised respect and deference to the power of a human thought. A human thought is a profoundly powerful event. It has been likened to a "speech not made," but nevertheless heard and felt in every corner and crevice of the host body, prompting a coincident bodily reaction that is chemical and immediate. This reaction can either impede or spur us on...the choice is ours.

Norman Cousins, the late editor of *The Saturday Review* magazine, was outspoken on the impact even individual words can have on our physiologies; words that when spoken, heard or thought can trigger a potential tidal wave of prerecorded feelings that our minds have long catalogued and associated with those words. If the magnitude of our bodily reaction can be softened or heightened based on selective wording, imagine the changes we can provoke and empower when we substitute entire replacement thoughts; thoughts that have been selected to stimulate our positive emotions and propel us forward towards a life of accomplishment and encouragement. Step-by-step, we can be free from the pulls of our past and the initiatives of others. More and more, we can become people whose lives are a product of choice and positive self-direction...our own!

Chapter 1

P.E.P. TALK
*P*reparation

Over the years, I've been asked to reflect on my experiences with the undefeated 1972 Dolphin team — to isolate the one factor that sticks out in my mind and best explains their success. On such occasions, I frequently resort to an analogy to impart my answer.

I suggest that the inquirer think back to his or her school days, picturing what class was like moments before a big test. We all experienced roughly the same thing. There were a number of students flipping through the book trying to cram in the eleventh hour, acknowledging to the world and to themselves they weren't well prepared. Then there was a somewhat smaller group of students sitting in a relaxed manner, confident in their knowledge and preparedness and eager to exhibit the fruits of that preparedness.

The Dolphins of 1972 were a monument to preparation...to a level of preparedness that warrants more than a cursory look so you can understand and appreciate its full impact. Yes, the players devoted hours to physical workouts and to classroom skull sessions. And yes, the players studied films and their unit's game plan until the desired moves and tactics became second nature. But so did the opposing teams. What separated the

Dolphins from the rest of the league that year went beyond luck, few injuries, and an easier-than-average schedule. What rose to the surface that year was the proverbial cream — the result of hours of extra work and extra sweat to achieve an edge over the competition...what Coach Shula called the "winning edge."

What sort of extra work? Basically, more of the same drills everyone else was doing along with a few designed to minimize turnovers — those culprit miscues on which a game can turn. One drill is still vivid in my mind. It was aimed at minimizing fumbles. During my visits to training camp, in the locker room after practice, I was struck by how these high-priced, best-of-the-best athletes were spending extra time on the basics. Bob Griese, the quarterback, would huddle with Larry Czonka, Jim Kiick and Mercury Morris, the running backs, and methodically and in slow motion go over the footwork and the timing of various hand-off patterns in the offensive scheme. Griese knew from experience there was no room for error, so extra time was taken to turn those handoffs into a well-practiced ballet. The result was evident in the team's statistics. The Dolphins were the least-penalized team in football and miscues in the backfield were virtually nonexistent. The Dolphins of 1972 were prepared ... period!

In addition to their finely honed executional precision on the playing field, the impact of all the discipline was even greater on the players' minds and hearts. It's as if the additive impact of all those drills — all the preparation — raised the team's and the individual players' level of preparedness beyond an uncharted threshold point. This threshold point, once exceeded, dissolved troublesome self-doubts and instilled an expectation of winning. It took me awhile to realize the operative dynamic at work here. This team just flat out BELIEVED. By passing the threshold point of exhaustive preparation, the team acquired what I call the "iasm" passkey which we'll discuss in Chapter 3. They were a walking billboard for everything we're about to discuss in the pages ahead.

There was very little arrogance and "in-your-face" celebration as the team methodically marched over their opponents and into the record books. A causal chain had been activated and due to the stability of the anchoring activities, the final link in the chain — winning the game on Sunday — became almost a foregone conclusion.

When you know in your heart you're doing what you love, are as well-prepared as time permits, and can sense the same level of commitment and involvement from those around and above you, an inner strength begins to grow. This inner strength can fortify and sustain you while those less dedicated and conditioned will fall prey to debilitating self-doubts, negative thoughts and fortitude fatigue.

The difference is not readily visible to the naked eye, but the impact on performance is unmistakable. It usually doesn't surface until crunch time, usually well into the second half. Many sportswriters attributed the Dolphins' strength in the closing minutes to their superior physical conditioning and double sessions of training in Miami's heat and humidity. There's no question the Dolphins' physical conditioning played an important role, but a far more powerful force was at work that season — a force that everyone overlooked as the uniqueness of the season unfolded and as students of the game began to conjecture and probe for the Dolphins' secret. I was also too caught up in the whirlwind to see clearly just what force — what glue — was holding the Dolphins' juggernaut together. The answer was as fundamental as the team's disciplined dedication to the fundamentals.

To a man, the Dolphins had a deep and abiding belief in themselves. Call it the "power of belief" if you like, but the Dolphins were simply not to be denied. Their self-doubt monsters were being held in check, under lock and key, and Don Shula was the jailer. Here was a man who ate, slept and dreamt football and although barely into his forties was already a legend in the making. When Don Shula entered a room, his command presence was palpable. When the coach told a rookie he was capable of more, by Shula's stature alone, the rookie came to believe.

When it came time for the exam to be distributed, the Dolphins as a team were amongst the group sitting quietly, eager to demonstrate for all their level of preparedness. With a coach who was even then judged to be the best in the business and with a system that was structured to squeeze out even the mention of the word failure, there was no room for complacency to get a toehold, much less a grip.

Although I traveled with the team, it took me some time to acquire the same level of belief that propelled the players. For me, the turning point came during the fourth quarter of a game with the Minnesota Vikings, number three in the string of seventeen consecutive victories that season. We were behind 14-9 with only 3 minutes to go in the game when Griese systematically began moving the team up the field. Just when the drive appeared to stall with third-and-long, Mercury Morris ran an end sweep, behind the thunderous blocking of Larry Little, for a 14-yard gain and a first down on the Viking 28-yard line. Merc was hit and turned backwards after a short gain, but miraculously kept his balance and actually gained the last six or seven yards running backwards and sideways in a manner that can only be described as inspired, if not possessed. In those 14 yards, I too became a believer and learned a valuable lesson about not losing heart and what disciplined execution is all about.

What does all this discussion about hours of practice, dedication and game day performance have to do with you and being successful in the 1990s? The answer...everything.

A chain of activities anchored the success of the Dolphins in 1972. Let's dissect those activities to extract the concepts that transcend football and apply to success in any field of endeavor. The members of the team had self-selected football as the most important thing in their lives at that moment. It was what they wanted and had committed to pursue. They weren't trying it out, they were doing it. They were initiators in life, not reactors. They had a goal — a dream — and they were living it. What may have appeared to be long hours to those less involved and less committed was experienced in far less severe terms by the players themselves. When the pursuit is a labor of love — when the involvement is one that stirs a passion and has you bounding out of bed in the morning in anticipation of the challenge that awaits — it's not hard work, it's what you want to be doing.

No one can advise you which field of endeavor will likely prompt that degree of involvement and ignite your inner fire. The answer has to flow from deep within you. We each have an applause meter buried deep inside. For some, multiple layers of calcified life experience have paved over the meter, rendering it virtually inaudible. These people first face the challenge of getting back in touch with their feelings...getting back in touch with themselves. Counseling is in order if the meter has been silenced. If the meter is still intact, the individual probably needs practice listening in and remembering to listen in. I would encourage such an individual to call a personal timeout and take a weekend off to get back in touch with him or herself. *The Me Encounter* provides just such an opportunity to reconnect. It transformed my life and could trigger a similar renaissance in yours as well.

What should be emerging from the haze is the notion that our first mission on the road to being a success in life is to make sure we've placed ourselves on the right playing field. There's only one person you can turn to for direction here and that's yourself. Despite the tendency in our society to look for the advice and counsel of experts, you are the only one who can determine the value of an experience for you. You are the only one who can assess the strength of your desire to pursue a job, a career or a relationship. You're the only one wired to your applause meter.

As Richard Nelson Bowles points out in *What Color Is Your Parachute*, desire is everything. "Your interests, wishes and happiness determine what you actually do well, more than your intelligence, aptitudes or skills do. Strength of desire outweighs everything else."[1]

All the answers you need are continuously being registered and displayed on your applause meter. You simply have to learn to "listen in."

Each of us carries around in our heart just such an applause meter; a built-in compass that can guide our every move if we haven't been conditioned to override it. It constantly measures our interest in what's happening around us. We differ only in how tuned in we are to its readings. If you came from a dysfunctional upbringing or if your feelings were infrequently acknowledged or affirmed as a child, chances are you learned to disregard or override your needle readings. Your meter is likely still operating, you've just conditioned yourself to avoid pain and disappointment by not paying attention to it. Not surprising if you grew up questioning your abilities, feeling left out, or just plain feeling "different." All the while, however, time has been slipping through your fingers.

Eventually we all come to realize our time is the only important earthly possession we have. Yet how often do we challenge how we use that time? Life is just a progression of "nows" but many of us fail to live in the present. Instead we rehash history and old hurts or needlessly worry about the future and how we'll handle it. What we miss is the joy of the moment and the exuberance we can feel as we make headway on an important goal.

We live in an age where much of our time gets chewed up for us. A recent study by a time management expert confirmed most people spend little time on things they value...like their families. The study found the average person in an average life span spends six months at stop lights, eight months opening junk mail, one year searching for lost objects, two years playing phone tag, four years doing housework, five years in line, and six years eating.

With only one life to live, it's time to grab hold of the piece that remains and make it the great adventure it was meant to be. It's time to begin to live like you mean it and to get your heart into it. No matter how much time has elapsed in your life, your mission is to get out front and lead the beautiful portion that remains. Dare I say there can be no more important matter on your plate at this time. None!

THE ACTION BEGINS IN YOUR MIND. How you think and behave and how you manage your time, are all learned habits...the result of conditioning. You are molded by your parents. Even the habit patterns you least admire you often unconsciously learn to imitate. Fortunately these tapes can be overridden and replaced. You start by becoming more aware of how you think, feel and act.

In psychotherapy sessions, significant attention and emphasis is placed on "feelings," particularly in orthodox, nondirective sessions. People are advised to listen to their feelings, to get in touch with them, to articulate and be guided by them. We are told that to deny or lose contact with our feelings is when we invite trouble. While this is accurate and sound advice, it is not the whole story. Yes, behavior follows feelings (as depicted in Figure 1), but there is a trap we can fall into if our analysis fails to source the origins of those feelings. Can we rely on our feelings to serve as an indicator of where we should be going in life?

Since many of the feelings we experience are not "fresh," but echoes from the past — triggered by an automatic thought, conversation, interpretation or an old unchallenged belief (see Figure 2) — they may not be valid indicators of where we should be going. Rather than keying off them as directional signposts, they may be symptoms that our triggering behaviors — our thoughts and prevalent conversations — need attention.

If we fail to source our feelings, we become captive to them. Captive to the inevitable behaviors they encourage. Negative thoughts and conversations may get triggered, which can retrigger and perpetuate the base feeling. Meanwhile, the culprit automatic thought or unchallenged belief lives on to contaminate our behavior again, that is, until we learn to intervene and disrupt the cycle and choose to anchor a new, causal chain with a more life-enhancing focus.

THE ACTION BEGINS IN YOUR MIND.

◆ ◆ ◆

Are you currently doing what you want to do in life, or what you feel you should be doing? Which is the case in your life now? Are you living in a way that is deeply satisfying to you, that allows you to give expression to your full range of interests and capabilities? Or are you marking time, waiting for your proverbial ship to come in or for some imagined, shadowy, big person — some surrogate parent — to rescue you in the eleventh hour and take charge of your life?

This next segment is entitled "Rocking Chairs and Wheelbarrows." See if the descriptions apply to you. I see people who mark time in a job, a career, or in a relationship that has lost its zip (or perhaps never had it in the first place), as being the occupants of a rocking chair. It offers them something to do at the moment but doesn't get them anyplace; doesn't help them to grow and to experience life as a continually unfolding adventure; doesn't help them to experience life as an act of creation unto itself, self-generating the energy and propulsion they need to continue moving forward.

With the passage of time, the underlying lack of fulfillment and stimulation eventually takes its toll, acting like a giant lid, slowly suffocating the bewildered hard workers below. If too much time elapses, we may be jolted awake one day, as life has a habit of doing, to find we're not only curled up in a rocking chair, but we've turned into a wheelbarrow in the process ... which is something that is useful only when pushed and is easily upset.

So again I ask, are you doing what you want to do in life, or what you feel you should be doing? I speak from experience when I say the "should do" voices can be very persuasive and hard to quiet. There are many rocking-chair inhabitants, myself only recently excluded, who have opted for this conformist role. Sadly, they are living a shallow, joyless life. They're not fully alive. They keep on keeping on because it seems to be what they "should" be doing.

There are two types of behaviors as indicated in Figure 3. The first, "self-initiated" and goal-directed, where we're moving forward against a goal that's important to us; and the second, "reactive" behaviors, where we're responding to someone else's goal-directed behavior. People with too high a share of reactive behavior are vulnerable to having their idle minds pulled down by negative, automatic thoughts. The lack of accomplishment and fulfillment that tends to surround reactive behavior is a breeding ground for resentment, blaming, and the "there's got to be more to life than this" lament.

The prescription to remedy this malady is not surprising. You've got to shift the mix to a higher proportion of initiated, goal-directed behavior, which is the subject of the next chapter.

Figure 1

Figure 2

♦ Attitudes/Beliefs
♦ Interpretations
♦ Prevalent Conversations
♦ Automatic Thoughts

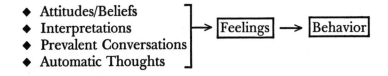

Figure 3

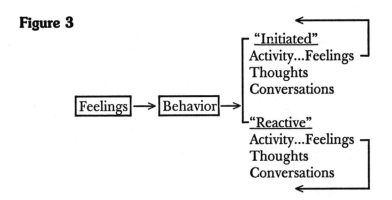

NOTE:
[1] Richard N. Bowles, *What Color is Your Parachute*, (Berkeley: Ten Speed Press, 1971), p.45.

Chapter 2

COMMITMENT & FOCUS

The late Dr. Maxwell Maltz, a noted plastic surgeon turned author and lecturer later in life, provided the inspiration for this chapter. In his book *Psycho-Cybernetics*,[1] Dr. Maltz likened the human brain and central nervous system to a homing torpedo. Both are success-driven mechanisms which require a target to function properly. Just as a homing torpedo fired without a target will wander aimlessly until its batteries wear down, so will we if we operate too long without a primary, compelling goal. Like the targetless torpedo, we can expect our batteries to wear down and eventually to be rendered dead in the water, suffering from a lack of propulsion and motivation. We'll have missed one of the fundamental truths — that the energy we lack needs to be replenished, and we do that through our accomplishments and achievements.

Time and time again you'll hear energy discussed as a key determinant to success, or conversely the reason why something didn't get done. "I just didn't have the energy." Sound familiar?

The intriguing thing about energy is that you can't procure it or find it. It is a byproduct of earlier decisions and commitments. Energy, just like meaning and purpose, is a gift you give yourself and you acquire it through your commitments.

Before you go any further, take a moment and make a short list of your commitments in life. What are they? Have you in fact made any yet? Are they commitments based on your own needle readings or commitments you inherited or acquired without adequate reflection?

The energy you seek must, of necessity, flow from your commitments and your involvements. It's as simple and as complex as that. If your energy level is wanting, you probably won't have to look any further than your goals and your commitments.

The Miami Dolphin team of 1972 had a clear and unshakeable goal: get to Super Bowl VII in Los Angeles and win. Their Cinderella season in 1971 had ended in disappointment at the hands of the Dallas Cowboys in Super Bowl VI. They had tasted the pageantry and the glory of qualifying for the big game and nothing short of proving themselves in the next edition in Los Angeles would suffice. Having experienced such a unanimity of purpose provided the individual and the organization with a decided leg up.

When a goal is publicly stated and embraced with that level of conviction, the subconscious mind is recruited to participate in the quest. The actual setting of the goal then becomes a milestone event. The assignment is not officially made to your subconscious until you give yourself permission to go for it — not try it, but to go for it. The significance of the "permission process" should not be dismissed as a stage you pass quickly through as you hurriedly gear up for the challenge ahead. Happily this will be the case for you, but often the permission process can become a formidable hurdle. For this reason, Chapter 6 will be devoted to helping you clear it with full knowledge of what's involved and what's at stake.

Richard Briley in his book *Are You Positive* likened the process of so embracing a goal that your subconscious is activated to dropping a large log on the bank at a river's bend.[2] As the river rushes by, silt and other debris gradually become trapped between the log and the bank. In time the whole contour of the river bend is altered. The same thing happens to your life when an important goal is put into place. You find you gravitate to certain conversations, magazines, TV programs and people. You join professional and social groupings where useful, goal-enhancing information is likely to be present. Much like the topography of the river bend, you find your life changing rather profoundly as your conscious and subconscious minds begin to seek out, sort through, and trap relevant information.

By dropping such a log in your life — by committing to a goal you feel passionately about — you begin to access an ancient wiring system that keeps you pointed and on course. Not only on course, but curiously and continuously encountering helpful material and people along the way. In his book *The Path Of Least Resistance*, Robert Fritz describes this creative process as being initiated by a vision. "The best place to begin the creative process is at the end."[3] In effect, picture in your mind the end result you're after before you get caught up contemplating how you'll get there. Once you hand the assignment to your subconscious — once you drop the log — you'll find the various pieces to the puzzle begin to organize themselves. Much of the creative process is improvisational and with your subconscious now engaged in the pursuit, it's not unusual to find the project will take on a life of its own. According to Fritz, "the resources you need somehow begin to gather themselves. The organic process (the creative process) may include unusual 'coincidences' that lead you directly to where you want to be."[4]

A good case in point is how the Dolphins came to pick up Earl Morrall after the Baltimore Colts put him on the waiver list during the 1971 season. I claim no involvement in the matter, other than having worked late that Friday night and having been the first in the office to see the routine waiver wire from the League Office. Except there was nothing routine about that particular wire. Buried in the middle was Earl Morrall's name. I called Joe Robbie, the Dolphins owner, at home. Joe acknowledged Earl had played for Coach Shula in Baltimore and that Don might indeed be interested. I called training camp as Robbie suggested and alerted Coach Shula's secretary to Earl's availability.

A few weeks later Earl was in town for a press conference announcing the Dolphins had successfully claimed him off waivers and signed him to a contract. What none of us knew at the time was how crucial the transaction would become to the team's fortunes six months later. Signing Earl Morrall was an expensive insurance policy, but one that paid off in spades during the fifth game of the ensuing season against the San Diego Chargers. The following is an excerpt from the Dolphins '72 yearbook.

> It was precisely 1:30 p.m., EDT, October 15, Game 5, the 14th play of the first quarter - and in the matter of a split second the entire season was to change for the Miami Dolphins, Bob Griese and Earl Morrall.
>
> Suddenly Griese was bringing his right arm back and looking downfield toward Jim Kiick while two members of the San Diego front four - Deacon Jones and Ron East - barrelled in. Almost all eyes moved from Griese to Kiick as the pass arched downfield. And when they returned upfield, Griese lay writhing in pain... The official diagnosis on Griese was a broken bone in his right ankle and a dislocation of the ankle. The unofficial diagnosis on Morrall was that the pressure was on.[5]

What a job this thirty-eight-year-old throwback from the crew-cut era did coming in cold to win that Charger game. Then, without missing a beat, he led the team through ten more victories, into the playoffs, and into the AFC Championship game before Griese was well enough to return. All this happened because Shula and Robbie shared a goal that was well-communicated, passionately embraced and that propelled each as they set about administering their respective ends of the business...and because Earl Morrall was living his dream and was prepared and ready.

The reason many of us fail to achieve our goals in life is that we either fail to set them in the first place or we never give ourselves permission to try, permission to get ready, or permission to extend our reach out beyond our current grasp. We follow the "should do" voices and never get the "iasm" passkey, a concept which we'll explore in the next chapter. The waste and frustration, on an individual and family level, is immense. On a national basis, the loss to the economy and to our national vigor is incalculable and staggering. John Greenleaf Whittier's words perhaps best sum up this tragedy of lost potential: "Of all sad words of tongue or pen, the saddest are these...(what) might have been."

Hopefully these words will strike a cord deep within you, spurring you on to pursue some goal or project that moves your applause meter smartly to the right. Let them help you to become less and less a person swayed by the initiatives of others and more and more a person whose life continually unfolds and blossoms like a flowering shrub; a shrub fertilized and pruned by your own thoughts and prevalent conversations, and watered the first thing every morning in accordance with the program to follow.

THE ACTION STARTS IN YOUR MIND.

NOTES:

[1] Dr. Maxwell Maltz, *Psycho-Cybernetics*, (New York: Simon & Schuster, 1960).

[2] Richard Briley, *Are You Positive*, (Washington, D.C.: Acropolis Books, 1986), p. 112.

[3] Robert Fritz, *The Path of Least Resistance*, (New York: Fawcett Columbine, 1989), p. 122.

[4] Ibid. p. 221.

[5] Miami Dolphins, Ltd., 1972 Dolphins Yearbook, p. 51.

Chapter 3

P.*E*.P. TALK
Enthusiasm

"Nothing great was ever achieved without enthusiasm."
-- Ralph Waldo Emerson

There's nothing quite like genuine enthusiasm. When you encounter it in a person it's hard not to be swayed. Like a smile, it has the ability to influence everyone in its path. It flows like a mighty river, with a swift and strong current, yet can soften those in its pull with its seductive and arresting sincerity.

One thing is certain about enthusiasm. Without it, you'll be hard pressed to muster the energy and the staying power you'll need to prevail over the inevitable failure messages the world will send you along the way. More importantly, the messages you send yourself will ultimately do you in.

Everything you've heard about enthusiasm being infectious is true and you can catch it. The secret is buried in the last four letters of the word — i.a.s.m. — I am sold myself. Until you really believe what you're doing is right for you, you won't possess the "iasm" passkey.

The 1972 Dolphins had a tremendous advantage in this regard. In addition to their own personal convictions that football was where they belonged, they had a powerful and daily rein-

29

forcement in the person of Don Shula. Over the years, I've come to realize just how significant and full of impact Coach Shula's presence was to the team's tempo and focus. He was the personification and embodiment of the dedication and commitment he demanded from his players. Over and above the football knowledge he brought to the table, the coach was a living model of his "winning edge" formula. He led his team by personal example, and what he exhibited was nothing short of a full-court press. His own consuming interest in improvement of self and his work was not lost on his players.

Shula's system demanded hard work, discipline and total dedication. He gave it himself and accepted nothing less from his players. His training-camp environment was a laboratory of classroom teaching and motivational psychology. The end result was a team of intensely motivated and dedicated men.

I believe a person reveals his or her own inner motivation and proclivities by the praise he or she renders to others. We can gain insight, therefore, into what drives Don Shula by what he once said to a Miami sportswriter about Vince Lombardi: "Lombardi was the best kind of teacher for he demanded discipline and gained it while imparting knowledge. To know how to do something but not having the discipline to do it at the right moment makes the knowledge itself a waste of time."[1] To this task of imparting knowledge and instilling discipline, Shula brings a strong, positive personality; the same kind of force the balance of this book will introduce into your life.

Few of you will be fortunate enough to have a Shula-like influence involved in your day-to-day life. Your objective in the pages that remain is to construct a program — a commercial — that will simulate a Shula-like presence, prompting and guiding your every move. As you've probably begun to suspect, **THE ACTION BEGINS IN YOUR MIND**...and the coach is going to be you.

I have addressed the importance of making certain you select the right playing field for you. Not one that pleases your parents, friends or spouse, but one that pleases you. As they say, you can't fool mother nature and you won't fool your heart of hearts. Way down deep you'll know if the fit is right. If your applause meter doesn't move briskly to the right on its own, no amount of coaxing or rationalizing is going to budge it. A given job, career or relationship may make infinite sense to the world at large, but if it doesn't move your needle...let the buyer beware. You're likely being sold a rocking chair.

I have witnessed a noticeable waning of enthusiasm in America in recent years, particularly in the service sector; an insidious and growing undertow pulling on the fabric of the American psyche as we enter the 1990s. While the Gulf War has given this country an infusion of renewed pride and identity, on an individual and spiritual level this prewar waning of enthusiasm — undocumented but nonetheless real and widely felt — continues unabated. A wholesale epidemic of what I call the "It's not my table" syndrome. You know what I mean. You've been seated in a restaurant for some time and finally catch the eye of the waiter or waitress only to be told "Sorry, it's not my table."

I understand from contacts in the outplacement business there's a growing motivational problem in corporate America as well. The destabilizing effect of all the merger and consolidation activity is sending out a wake-up call; a call being heard largely by rocking-chair occupants who have deferred to a conformist role and have been going through the motions for years. These people, as Robert Fritz suggests in *The Path Of Least Resistance*, were conditioned early to monitor the "circumstances" in life and to respond or react accordingly. With the circumstances of corporate life changing, they're now questioning the appropriate response, consistent with what Fritz labels their "reactive-responsive orientation."[2]

To break free from a life of reactive problem solving and oscillation, you must first learn to listen in. My assumption is you have already, either because your applause meter is hard wired to your consciousness, you've benefitted from counseling, or you've read *The Me Encounter*. You know what you want to accomplish...what you want to become.

But knowing where you want to go and getting there can be two distinctly separate challenges. As Will Rogers points out: "Even if you're on the right track, you'll get run over if you just sit there."

Considerable attention is given in today's self-help literature to the concept of "congruence." A state-of-being where what we are thinking, feeling and doing become uniform and converge and coincide with our experiences and our awareness. The more congruent we are in a given communication, the more able we are to listen accurately to the reply...to really "meet" another. If a job or relationship prompts us to say things we're not truly feeling, we'll be forced to use defenses to keep unwanted feelings away. These defenses take time and energy to sustain; time and energy that could be used to further our growth. Since our inner feelings are the wellspring of our energy and creativity, if we stifle them we're actually placing a big lid over our future growth. We are cutting ourselves off from our core — from our true identity — and the unbounded energy that lies dormant there.

You, too, can tap into your own energy geyser, but it won't happen if you wait for the circumstances to be just right...for your proverbial ship to come in. No one is going to walk into your life with a placard that says "Okay _____, now is the time to do it." Your ship is out there, but you're going to have to swim out to it.

Not surprisingly, **THE ACTION STARTS IN YOUR MIND** ... and the starting point is the most important minute of your life ... which is fast approaching.

As you no doubt have learned, you can't manufacture or fake enthusiasm for long. It's a byproduct of deciding to move in conformity with your feelings — your needle readings — and then committing to that change. Then and only then will you have the "iasm" passkey. Then and only then will you be in congruence and be able to muster the strength to strive.

NOTES:
[1] Morris McLemore, *The Miami Dolphins*, (Garden City: Doubleday & Co., 1972), p. 124.
[2] Robert Fritz, *The Path of Least Resistance*, (New York: Fawcett Columbine, 1989), p. 18.

Chapter 4

VISUALIZATION & SELF-TALK

Our discussion of enthusiasm would not be complete without re-emphasizing the role "belief" plays in the whole dynamic. For our purposes, the "iasm" passkey and the power of belief are one and the same. As our friends at American Express advise, "Don't leave home without them." You'll just be marking time.

If you doubt the power of belief, consider the following phenomenons. The placebo effect often observed in the medical world is a good example of getting better because you believe you should. The same holds for Black Magic. Those who are affected and influenced by the spells are affected because they believe in it. Another example is hypnosis. People under hypnosis believe completely what they are told. If told a plate weighs 2000 pounds, they will be unable to budge it, even if it weighs only a few ounces. The power of belief is that strong.

Normally you believe what you experience. Your confidence level is built by taking action and seeing that action produce the desired result. In other words, your actions precede and cause your belief. You might be thinking, "that's all well and good but how do I break into something new and muster the power of belief if I haven't done it yet or, worse, tried and failed?" It's an excellent question. The answer is what this chapter is all about. You do it through guided visualization and affirmative self-talk, the component activities that will comprise your commercial-to-be.

The past twenty years have witnessed a virtual explosion of physical fitness in the United States. More and more people are out exercising: fellow joggers, bikers and walkers. The streets are far from crowded, but the trend is evident. We have become a country of "conditioners" *but* we're only doing half the job. We're working on half the system — our bodies — to the exclusion of our minds. Our commercials will make up for this imbalance.

We seem to have lost sight of something the ancient Chinese had great respect for — the mind-body link. Without understanding the chemistry of the linkage, early Chinese doctors often played the role of mental cheerleader. Unlike our medical system where we pay doctors when we're sick to make us better, the ancients focused on preventive medicine and paid their doctors every day they were well. They stopped payment when they were ill, the opposite of our approach. The Chinese doctors of old may not have understood the connective neuronal pathways between the mind and body, but that didn't impede their acting on their intuition. They fed and nourished their minds on a daily basis. We need to do likewise.

The "signals" to do so have likely been there for some time — the mental signals I mean. We're familiar with certain bodily signals. Hunger pains indicate its time to eat. Tight clothes are a warning to cut our caloric intake. Easily fatigued and short of breath tells us it's time to exercise and build up our stamina. But how many of us have learned to tune in to our minds? How many of us have been alerted to know the signals that indicate it's mental nourishment time? The signals are unmistakable: low energy, lost zest, hopelessness, anxiety, insomnia, malaise...in a word, depression.

The medical community is still awakening to the chemical complexity of the human body, particularly the human mind. Much of the havoc wrought on the body by stress is initiated by a mental process — how we interpret events around us and the meaning we attach to them. With stress causing or accelerating from 70% to 90% of all medical complaints, stress maintenance and reduction programs are certainly essential. But, they must not be our remedial focal point. With stress largely self-imposed (the result of our interpretations), much of our recovery and preventive efforts must go against the root cause — our thoughts. We need to anchor a new, causal chain...a chain with a more life-enhancing focus. In essence, our automatic thoughts get us into the stressful state and our replacement thoughts can get us out, and keep us out.

Our understanding of the chemistry of a human thought and its reverberative effect on the host body will be rounded out in time. What's important to acknowledge is that the chain is triggered by a thought, with our tendency to interpret intent a leading example.

The emergency response — often called "fight or flight" — is a hereditary protective mechanism that was originally for physical threats. Today, we trigger it needlessly in response to mental and emotional stresses and challenges. The resulting chemical changes in our body have a ripple effect that can take it's toll. When the emergency response is triggered, adrenaline is secreted. If chronically activated, the pituitary gland secretes a hormone called ACTH which causes the outer layer of the adrenal cortex to secrete hormones called steroids to prevent inflammation. The problem is, it's an excessive and inappropriate reaction of the body's defense system to a nonphysical stressor. If it persists, the unrelenting release of hormones can cause exhaustion, ulcers and kidney damage, and eventually a heart attack from the continued presence of adrenaline. Adrenaline raises blood pressure, heart rate and can promote the use of a passing glob of cholesterol to quick fix the inevitable tiny tears in artery linings induced by today's active lifestyles. Thus, chronic stress can kill, unless we learn to interrupt and disrupt the causal chain, which is what this book is all about.

THE ACTION BEGINS IN YOUR MIND

◆ ◆ ◆

ADJUSTMENT

We won't advance too far against any goal until we learn the art of adjusting and are prepared to do our part. A short, humorous story lends support.

While assigned to West Point pack in the late 1960s, I had the pleasure of working for a thoughtful, nice man. A breath of fresh air from previous employment relationships, Colonel Bill Crim had a penchant for making work fun. Although we had little in common, we grew to share a mutual fondness and respect. I was particularly fond of Colonel Crim's good-natured style of kidding and poking fun.

Back in those days the Army football team was struggling. The Vietnam War had hurt the Academy's ability to recruit blue-chip athletes and the caliber of players and team depth was not up to the onerous schedule. Schedules were often set years in advance and the games back then were remnants of the Paul Dietzel era, when Dietzel dreamed of restoring Army as a national football power. Coach Tom Cahill had the unhappy task of taking his undermanned teams against the likes of Oklahoma, Missouri and Notre Dame.

Colonel Crim was the ticket manager for Army at the time and I was his assistant. After watching a particularly lopsided game, Crim appeared in the ticket office eager to share a newfound insight. "I finally figured out what Coach Cahill's strategy is," Crim remarked with his customary mischievous twinkle. "He uses the first series of plays to find out what doesn't work, then he surprises the opponent by running them all game."

With apologies to Tom Cahill, who was a far better coach than his Dietzel-sabotaged record indicated, the point of the story is simple. Only when we stop doing what doesn't work can things get better. Adjustment is the name of the game. One of the best places to effect such adjustment is in the inner world of our thoughts — managing and influencing our thoughts through guided visualizations and self-talk...the power of suggestion, self-imposed. And the best time to begin is the first minute each morning, the most influential minute of the day.

Rudyard Kipling was dancing on the edges of this very notion when he wrote about the unforgiving minute: "If you can fill the unforgiving minute, yours is the earth and everything that's in it." Cognitive therapists have long held that many, if not all, of our least-liked behaviors, and the feelings that trigger them, are themselves triggered by automatic thoughts — automatic thoughts that race through our minds seemingly uncontested; thoughts that gained residence and established a beachhead in our neuronal pathways often as a result of childhood experiences and conditioning. Whether valid or not, these thoughts endure and form the bedrock of our attitudes and beliefs, which in turn serve as our mental and emotional software, dictating how our experiences and perceptions will be processed and interpreted.

If our beliefs and attitudes remain frozen and beyond examination, personal growth will stagnate. The unforgiving minutes of our life will be filled by default, not managed. An endless stream of automatic thoughts — echoes from our past — will live on and tighten their grip on our consciousness, limiting our possibilities in the process.

The solution is to recognize and to seize each day the many opportunities to influence these thoughts — and the feelings they trigger — by seeding replacement, life-enhancing thoughts at key moments. The most propitious moment — the focal point of your new self-actualization program — is, coincidentally, the most important minute in your life...the first minute every morning. As John Keats once said, "Well begun is half done."

The glue that holds the program together is something called "synaptic efficacy" (a property of the brain we'll review in Chapter 8) which explains how thoughts become etched and imprinted in our minds — through repetition — and how they fade from disuse.

The agent of change — the applier of the synaptic efficacy glue — remains throughout YOU. There's no escaping the role you must play. Consider the case of Mario.

Mario was a middle-aged man of modest means, born and bred in New York City. He kept to himself and was a law-abiding citizen. He dreamed of one day enjoying great wealth and social position. With the advent of the N.Y. Lottery, he allowed those distant dreams to move in closer on the horizon. Within a short time, Mario became convinced he was going to win. The big drawing was only days away. Being a religious man, Mario prayed constantly for God to intercede. Over the years Mario felt he had developed a close relationship with God. Considering all the prayers and candles he had lit, Mario's confidence was sky high. When the winner was announced and someone else won, Mario was devastated, but not defeated. He figured God had his reasons so he marked the next drawing date on the calendar and vowed to double his prayers and the number of candles lit. When the big moment came and again his name was not called, Mario couldn't contain his disappointment. In a rare burst of emotion, he thrust his eyes skyward and demanded an explanation. This time Mario found God far more responsive. Surrounded by a crack of thunder, the words reverberated down to earth: "MARIO...BUY A TICKET!"

The message is clear. We have to do our part. We have to buy a ticket, and...**THE ACTION BEGINS IN YOUR MIND.**

No doubt you're familiar with Thomas Edison's famous remark that success or genius is 1% inspiration and 99% perspiration. I believe Edison was directionally right but off in his math. Considering the role visualization and the right side of the brain can play, it's probably more like a 40/60 split. But no matter how you cut it, there are no short cuts — you have to put in the time and effort.

There is no such thing as "staying even" in life. There was a sign in the West Point gym on this very point. Located alongside the indoor track, you could reflect on it lap after lap. It read, "If you're not improving, you're deteriorating."

If you're beginning to think "this sounds like too much work," the program has a hidden benefit. A funny thing happens when you finally find a goal and an involvement that match your inner feelings and proclivities. Your whole being comes alive and you're drawn to the activity. The hours you devote may seem excessive to the uninitiated, but to you they fly by. This isn't work as you used to know it, this is home. This is what you were meant to do.

Dr. Maxwell Maltz, the noted plastic surgeon I spoke of earlier, provides the last puzzle piece before I get into the details of assembling your commercial. As his practice progressed, Dr. Maltz was struck by how, when he changed a man's face, he often changed the inner man as well. He found his incisions cut more than skin deep, often penetrating deep into the client's psyche as well. He felt compelled to understand this phenomenon and soon became quite an expert on the self-image and the role self-image plays in life.

He learned most from the patients whose personality and behavior failed to change after the disfiguring physical features had been removed. Dr. Maltz identified the self-image as the key to human personality and human behavior. "Change the self-image and you change the personality and the behavior...The self-image sets the boundaries of individual accomplishment. It defines what you can and cannot do. Expand the self-image and you expand the 'area of the possible.'"[1]

Dr. Maltz concluded that "experiencing" was the key; that confidence and self-image are derived from real-life action. He was intrigued by the growing evidence that the human brain and central nervous system operate according to the principles of Cybernetics...in a purposeful, goal-directed fashion. His breakthrough came when he realized the human mind not only can manufacture experience, literally create it in our mind's eye, but that the central nervous system can't tell the difference between an "actual" experience and the experience that we vividly imagine.

Dr. Maltz was an early proponent of visualization. He wrote that "a human being always acts and feels and performs in accordance with what he imagines to be true about himself."[2] In much the same way that a hypnotized subject acts out the hypnotist's suggestion, Maltz concluded that our visualizations gradually add to our self-image and eventually to our expectations. To the extent we can push for "details" in our mental pictures, the exercise is received as a real practice experience by our minds. With each mental rehearsal — with each airing of our commercial — we are dropping additional logs on our rapidly changing river bank. Gradually our confidence builds as we open up space in our lives for the envisioned events to actually take place.

We've touched on the role our attitudes and beliefs play in

shaping our preconceptions and the near tyrannical hold these preconceptions have over what we "see." The preconceptions drive our expectations and like clockwork we get what we expect. It all traces to the principle belief of the Transactional Analysis folks that early in life we choose a central emotional position, such as I'm Not Okay — You're Okay. This position becomes the affective position we tend to return to over and over because all our experience is selectively interpreted to support it. What Maltz knew and described as our self-image is what Transactional Analysis refers to as the central emotional position. Since all of life is selectively interpreted to support that position — that self-image — we act, feel and behave in strict accordance with the sort of person we conceive ourselves to be. The early signals of our worth and our capabilities that we receive from parents, teachers, coaches and friends often form an intricate pattern of mental fences that can constrain us. Mental handcuffs that are placed on us early in life can hold us back for a lifetime — a lifetime of lost potential — if we fail to disprove or challenge them. Their hold over us is vise-like because we come to "believe" in their validity. Through repetition of the underlying limiting automatic thoughts over time, we condition ourselves to believe it. Fortunately, the same process can be employed to undo the damage. By changing what we think about, talk about and visualize, we change what we believe, expect and, in time, what we become.

THE ACTION STARTS IN YOUR MIND.

Learning the visualization technique is easy. Many of you are versed in its use in a negative way — when you worry. You think into the future and dwell on one or more negative outcomes. As the negative picture in your mind comes into sharper focus, you may find your palms are sweating and your pulse has quickened. Nothing bad has happened yet except in your mind, but the queasy, nervous feeling in your stomach is real. It's 100% pure anxiety and its 100% self-manufactured. Such is the power of a human thought — ample evidence unto itself of the mind-body link.

Fortunately the linkage works equally well on the positive side. By getting back in touch with past moments of accomplishment and personal success, you can relive those marvelous feelings of elation and triumph, triggering the release of energy and exuberance much like you experienced at the original event.

To this point, Dr. Wilder Penfield, past director of the Montreal Neurological Institute, discovered thirty years ago that the human brain functions like a tape recorder, recording both the individual's perception of an event *and* the exact feelings and sensory input experienced at the moment as well. Penfield came upon this finding when performing a brain operation while the patient was still awake. When Penfield happened to touch an area of the cortex with a small probe, the patient remarked how she was instantly "reliving" an incident from her childhood, an incident she had forgotten. Now that it was triggered, she was not so much remembering it as she was actually reliving the moment, to include all the sights, sounds and original sensory sensations.

One word of caution. What is brought back into consciousness is not an exact re-enactment of the event but rather a re-enactment of what you perceived and interpreted. The feelings triggered by that initial interpretation were recorded also and they come flooding back as part of the event memory. The reason for caution is to not interpret the presence of a strong feeling now as being an accurate reading of what happened then or of your current inner state now. It can simply mean your tape-recorder mind is functioning efficiently, triggering one or more automatic thoughts to flash through your mind. Often the thoughts go unnoticed but the feelings recorded with them get released and quickly make their presence known.

For this reason, we need to embrace the opportunity and the responsibility to manage and influence our thoughts in a direction and in a manner that will help mold and foster a healthier sense of self. We need to think healthier, tapping into the bodily rewards of thinking and feeling like a winner. The bodily penalties for not doing so can take the form of any of the stress-induced ailments we described earlier — headaches, backaches, ulcers, and neck and shoulder stiffness to name a few. When we're experiencing these discomforts, chances are something we've been thinking, feeling or saying is inconsistent with our inner reality and truth. We're not in congruence and our vigor and creativity will suffer until we remedy the imbalance.

THE ACTION BEGINS IN YOUR MIND

Central to Dr. Maltz's findings is the notion that man is by nature a goal-striving being. That what many call the "subconscious mind" is really a goal-striving creative mechanism — a mechanism that we activate by "visualizing" in our conscious mind what we want to achieve. The science of Cybernetics regards the brain and central nervous system as an automatic goal-seeking machine which uses feedback and stored information to converge on a goal. The setting and placement of the goal becomes critical since our goal-seeking mechanism is inoperable without it. We place the goal deep into our psyche — engaging the ancient wiring system we spoke of earlier — by actively visualizing the attainment of our goal. Here's how it's done.

VISUALIZATION

You've been doing it all your life. Daydreaming is a prime example. Who, as a youngster, hasn't indulged in a fantasy or two in which they played a starring role. Perhaps you were the Homecoming Queen or hit the deciding home run for the city championship. This "theater in your mind" operates on no particular schedule; generally, whenever the mood strikes or when boredom encourages you to check-out mentally. No one receives instruction on how to do it. In fact, many of us have been reprimanded for indulging in it when it interfered with what was being asked of us at the moment.

We're going to dust off your daydreaming mechanism of old and commission it to think about very specific events. Events that depict you in the process of attaining and revelling in the goal or goals you'll be capturing on paper in a subsequent chapter. The reason is simple. What you creatively imagine in your mind sets the "goal picture" that your automatic success mechanism — your subconscious — locks onto. In order for the homing mechanism to operate, there has to be a goal in sight. Using visualization is a continuation of how we learned to walk, throw a ball, even how to stand in the kitchen. We learned from watching others. From repeatedly holding those images in our minds, something seems to get programmed and we find in time we are able to replicate the motion(s).

Our minds and bodies are capable of a tremendous range of activity if we don't encumber them. No one purposely limits themselves but that's exactly what we do when we fail to challenge certain performance-related beliefs, particularly those acquired early in life. These beliefs truly set the boundaries within which our activities — our lives — dutifully and obediently comply. What arbitrary limitations do you suppose you've been living with needlessly all these years?

In spite of best intentions, important people around us may say things that were never intended to be cast in stone yet get fixed in our young minds. The damage can be across a broad front. Consider these seemingly harmless observations, perhaps uttered at the time just to make conversation:

"Dave is our student, not our athlete." (or vice versa)
"Peter is our shy one."
"Diane is really bright but has no common sense."
"Lauren is not a whiz in math."
"Brian is going to drive me crazy."

These statements pale in comparison to what is said in abusive households and what isn't said like "you're a special person with very special qualities — I love you."

Your intent in the pages that follow will be to generate a number of replacement thoughts — affirmative in nature — that you'll substitute for those that have impeded your growth in the past. These thoughts will comprise the narrative portion of your commercial.

Let's conclude our background discussion on visualization by looking at an area where it has become an accepted path to improved performance — the world of sports. Sports psychologists are convinced the difference between winning and losing for high-performance athletes is largely a mental difference. The objective is to liberate the athletes from their mental or emotional obstacles, giving them an edge on the competition. By visualizing a perfect performance and triggering positive emotions in the body, the fear of failure recedes along with the tendency to become tentative and to stiffen up. Feelings of confidence grow from the simulated performance previewed in the mind. The individual's ability to mimic the motions so pictured also grows in time.

Steven DeVore, creator of Syber Vision, describes this phenomenon as it relates to motor skills as follows: "Syber Vision is based on a phenomenon of motor skills called modeling. You observe someone who performs at a highly efficient level and you get a kinesthetic response in which your body feels the sense of movement. You convert the information from visual to motor memory."[3]

A kinesthetic response is a sensory experience of end organs located in muscles, tendons and joints. By repeatedly viewing a videotaped movement, our end organs begin to get the picture and can begin to mimic the movement. This suggests that imagery can enhance the cognitive aspects of learning or polishing a skill while actual practice can ensure the motor aspects progress in sync.

Our goal is getting you to create a Syber Vision-like commercial in your mind of you achieving your most coveted goal. To ensure the image connects with the ancient wiring system intuited by Dr. Maltz, you'll picture the setting with as much graphic detail as possible. You'll stay with the image until you feel yourself responding physically and emotionally to the pictured event.

Let's begin. A good warm-up is to reflect back on your most vivid past success. Get into a quiet place and make yourself comfortable, but remain seated upright. Close your eyes and let your body go limp. If you meditate, your make-ready routine is ideal. Once you feel your body settle down and your breathing relax, you're ready to begin. Let your thoughts drift back to that happy moment. See yourself back then, alive in that moment as if viewing a home movie of the event. Scan the scene, noting the detail — what you and those around you are wearing, doing and saying. As you get back in touch with this memory, you should begin to feel rumblings of the same positive emotions that likely overwhelmed you at the time. Embrace the feelings as they return. Get a sense of the underlying confidence and energy that accompany them. Remember how full and rich life seemed when you had that sense of accomplishment. Most of all, remember how positive you felt about yourself.

Take a moment right now and perform this visualization. Stay with it until you re-experience the glow and the surge of those winning feelings.

◆ ◆ ◆

As you open your eyes and return to the present, realize what you have just done. In less time than you might have previously thought possible — likely less than one minute — you've reminded yourself "up close and personal" what it feels like to be a winner. And remember, this little trip down memory lane was orchestrated entirely by YOU...the direct result of a conscious decision to think a particular thought.

With this heightened awareness of the power of your own thoughts, what better time than right now to commit to better managing your thoughts in the future; to think about changing what you *choose* to think about; to giving your One Minute P.E.P. Talk the twenty-one day investment called for and to committing to do it, not just to try it.

Those who have read *The Me Encounter* will recall the biblical story of Lazarus rising from the dead. The point learned by Mario is much the same — we have to buy a ticket:

> Guarding and blocking the entrance to Lazarus'
> tomb was a large stone. Jesus was deeply moved
> by the pain of Mary and Martha, Lazarus's sisters,
> and asked those assembled to "take away the stone."
> Moving the stone himself would have been a minor
> event compared to raising Lazarus from the dead,

but Jesus insisted those present put forth some effort too.

We all likely have stones holding back miracles in our own lives. Stones of self-doubt, unforgiveness or disbelief. As you approach the opportunity about to unfold here, view it as an opportunity to regain control of your life. An opportunity to put forth an effort — a uniquely personal effort — to "take away the stone" that may be blocking your forward progress, preventing you from becoming the person you were meant to be.

THE ACTION BEGINS IN YOUR MIND.

NOTES:
[1] Dr. Maxwell Maltz, *Psycho-Cybernetics*, (New York: Simon & Schuster, 1960), p. ix.
[2] Ibid. p. 28.
[3] Steven DeVore, The Syber Vision Catalog, Spring 1986, p.4.

Chapter 5

STRIVING & WINNING

"It is in the process of attainment that we thrive."
-- Paul Kurtz *Exuberance-A Philosophy of Happiness*

I call it the Big Deception — the notion that happiness can be driven, purchased or worn; that happiness is something we experience while engaged as a consumer.

It is not my intent to discredit Madison Avenue and the marketing profession. Humans are aspirational in nature and it is inevitable that an ever-growing range of merchandise would be offered to help satisfy those hungers. What doesn't get mentioned in the ads is that the so called "good life" can be empty and lacking in fulfillment.

Paul Kurtz in his book *Exuberance-A Philosophy of Happiness* places rightful emphasis on the journey and the act of striving itself. Kurtz feels we are our happiest when making headway on a goal that is important to us. "It is in the process of attainment that we thrive."[1]

Jeffrey Keith, a twenty-seven-year-old who lost a leg to cancer, is a living example of the truth of Kurtz's words. Jeffrey's story is similar to that of Terry Fox. Perhaps you saw the movie on television. Fox lost a leg to cancer and died in 1981 while attempting to run across Canada on one leg. Keith was similarly inspired to prove himself still capable, and in 1985 became the first to run across the United States from Boston to Los Angeles on one leg. It took him eight months of running from six to eight hours a day, but he made it. Keith now travels to companies across the nation to give motivational talks on the "Power of Purpose."

"Everyday I got up and knew I had to run eighteen miles a day," he remembers. "There were some days when I woke up and thought about how numb my leg would get, the cold, the sores on my leg, and I wanted to turn back. I would let these things — fear and apprehension — get into my head and I almost couldn't do it."

Keith figured after he completed the run he'd just go back to work. He didn't anticipate people would want to hear his story. "The funny thing is that through all the pain during the run, I was happiest because I had a purpose and was helping people." Keith raised over one million dollars for the American Cancer Society as a result of his run.

When was the last time you bounded out of bed in the morning with a sense of purpose like Keith's? As Helen Keller once said from her dark, silent, contemplative world, "Life is either a great adventure or it's nothing." What might you do to add an element of adventure to your life? You might be surprised to find a simple change of outlook is all that's needed; a change in where you let your prevalent thoughts go.

As you no doubt have surmised, **THE ACTION BEGINS IN YOUR MIND.**

◆ ◆ ◆

Striving is a two-part movement. First, set a goal that's right for you and second, steadfastly stay the course. The glue that holds the two together we've already discussed — commitment. Our focal point here will be the effort required, but first a few words on our national preoccupation with winning.

WINNING

> "Upon these fields of friendly strife
> are sown the seeds,
> which on other fields
> and other days
> will bear the fruits of victory"
> -- General Douglas MacArthur
> Michie Stadium Plaque - West Point

The whole world loves a lover, but in the United States it is the winner who commands the spotlight. Our uniquely American culture places a strong premium on individual effort, personal accomplishment and spirited competition. It's not surprising a country built on these principles would become entranced by the world of sports. We have a natural attraction to the underdog and an insatiable appetite for witnessing the triumph of the human spirit over insurmountable odds. Nowhere has this national trait been more evident, or perhaps more exploited, than in the phenomenal box office success of the *Rocky* movies. The more complicated the world becomes, the more we seem to thrive on reassuring examples that raw dedication and hard work will prevail in the end. Perhaps that's it in a word, we find it all very "reassuring."

Early in childhood we learn that we live in a world of measurement. It starts when we're moments old, with our birth weight and body length. Our parents track how soon we walk, talk and become toilet trained. At some point we catch on and join in, keeping a close watch on our height and weight. For awhile it seems our impact on the world will be a function of our size. Our performance in school is continually measured and graded. It doesn't take too many report cards to realize this is the program. We live in a world of continual measurement and evaluation.

Even in childhood sporting events there's the ever-present threat or question of measurement. How many hits did you get, how many times at bat, how many points did you score, what place did you finish, how did the judges score you? With all this measurement and the pressures that can build, it's not surprising a viewpoint would emerge condemning our emphasis on winning as excessive.

You're familiar with the central argument. On one side are those who feel "if it wasn't important we wouldn't keep score" and on the other side are those who feel the pressure to excel and perform can so surround children that they might succumb to a life of detachment and withdrawal or worse.

I believe the solution to this timeless argument is embodied in the words General Douglas MacArthur used to describe the athletic fields at West Point. It bears repeating:

> "Upon these fields of friendly strife
> are sown the seeds
> which on other fields
> and other days
> will bear the fruits of victory"

MacArthur understood that the qualities which make the difference on a battlefield are the same as those learned on the fields of friendly strife — the playgrounds of our youth and adolescence. The orientation to planning, training, teamwork and execution are evident in both spheres. What may not be evident is that special quality of inner strength and conviction that the athlete acquires after hours of practice and preparation; an inner reserve that can be called forth and drawn upon when others are feeling the pull of self-doubt and fatigue. When the occasion calls for continued effort and fatigue has taken its toll, this element of conditioning comes to the fore. It's a function of intensifying your preparations and marshalling your energies to surpass that threshold point we spoke of earlier, the point where you come to believe — really believe — you can do it.

In the context of the battlefield or professional sports arena, no one would argue the importance of training, discipline and hard work. Where things get muddled is when we shift our gaze to the little league field or to the office. At what point does winning give way to other desirable outcomes? I believe the answer is a matter of common sense and personal value judgments. Take little league baseball for example. Who would argue against the notion that the overriding reason to play little league is to have fun, to learn the fundamentals of teamwork and to build self-esteem and character.

Yet we've all witnessed or heard about coaches and parents who want to impose a "winning is everything" mentality at that level. These are situations where the adult's ego fulfillment gets in the way of the program's intended purpose. There's a time and place for everything. We have only to reflect on the reason for the activity in the first place to know the appropriate intensity to be expected and encouraged.

Winning is far from overrated. In fact, it's essential to a healthy self-image. Winners learn to stretch themselves, to be able to reach down for that little extra when others have already mentally gone to the showers. Winning builds confidence, morale and the development of "can do" attitudes for later in life. For this reason, it is important that educators supply ample opportunity for young people to experience achievement early in their schooling. Encouraging and nurturing an attitude of striving and reaching is a gift more valuable than gold. As John Townsend Trowbridge once said, "Not in rewards, but in the strength to strive, the blessing lies."

Vince Lombardi had an answer to this dilemma of winning that is instructive. Lombardi was well-acquainted with the positive emotions that accompany a win. He also knew the crippling and debilitating negative emotions that a loss could trigger. Lombardi's secret was simple and ingenious. In his mind, he never allowed himself to lose. "I never lost a game...I've just run out of time."

By remaining convinced he only lacked time, Lombardi was able to maintain the self-image of a winner, thereby avoiding the downward pull of a loss taken to heart. Perhaps the adage, "It's not whether you win or lose but how you play the game" should be modified to read "It's not whether you win or lose but how you interpret the result." Once again, the power of our thoughts over our emotions and the notion that how we end up feeling is directly tied to what we permit ourselves to think.

The ability to turn a loss into a win is simply a matter of interpretation. It's all in your head. Rather than focus on the gap on the scoreboard, think about the things you did right. Isolate the areas of evident progress and give yourself credit and a pat on the back — what Dr. Irene Kassorla calls a "mental hug."

THE ACTION BEGINS IN YOUR MIND.

Life typically doesn't give you what you want, only what you'll accept. The secret is not to accept a negative outcome. You are never defeated until you stop trying or decide the quest is over. Pavlov's "gradualness" comes into play here. You need time to grow and time to learn; time to explore and stretch your abilities; operating room where falling short is not an infrequent occurrence and part of the learning process that empowers growth. It all depends on your frame of mind and how you're inclined to interpret the result.

Once again, **THE ACTION BEGINS IN YOUR MIND.**

NOTES:

[1] Paul Kurtz, *Exuberance - A Philosophy of Happiness*, (Buffalo: Prometheus Books, 1977), p. 175.

[2] Dr. Irene Kassorla, *Go For It*, (New York: Delacorte Press, 1984), p. 103.

Chapter 6

P.E.**P**. TALK
*P*ermission

Giving yourself permission to do something seems simple enough. Yet it can be a complex process wherein the coveted brass ring — permission to pull out all the stops — is often within sight, occasionally even grasped, but not fully owned and possessed for some time. My intent is not to dissuade you but to prepare you for a possible challenge. Forewarned is forearmed.

The greater the departure a new goal represents from our current orbit of activities, the greater the likelihood we may encounter a permission problem. I believe the reason for this is rooted in our culture. From the time we reach the age of reason to well into our twenties, most of us have been in pursuit of credentials and institutionalized approval. Our graduation from grammar school authorized our movement into high school and a high school degree was required to move on to college. In each case a credential was received and the granting of the credential was often surrounded by ritual and ceremony. Along the way, we may have become conditioned to expect and require such ceremony — such permission giving — before we moved to the next stage and could believe we had qualified and were officially ready.

For awhile in our lives, such passage points come every four years. They're built into the educational system and happen automatically. We merely have to meet the requirements and the forward march continues.

Armed with our latest education credential and fresh from a graduation ceremony, we enter the world of work. It's not uncommon to then enter one or more training programs and to receive attendance certificates, qualifying us for still further movement and promotion.

In each case, we defer to some outside authority to punch our ticket and authorize our advancement. Then a strange thing happens. Once the entry experience and the honeymoon are over, there are no more institutionalized checkpoints; no more wake-up calls that come along every four years to boot us forward. All change beyond this point must flow from us...and that's the rub. Most of us, by then, have had precious little experience at self-initiated change. The institutions that guided our youth have seen to it.

Compounding this scenario is the plight of the person who sociologist John Reisman labeled "other directed." These people so seek the approval and acceptance of others that they lose touch with their own applause meter. They look for a consensus of opinion and fail to give proper weight to their own. This may account for why a number of people are influenced and coaxed into rocking-chair careers or jobs, and why for many the next wake up call may not come for years, often taking the form of a jolt or a loss. The death of a loved one, getting divorced or fired, losing one's health or having it threatened, are lead candidates. Perhaps one of these alarm clocks has recently gone off in your life. Whatever your circumstances, your presence here makes a strong statement...you've decided to buy a ticket. You've decided to make some changes.

Any discussion of permission would be incomplete without getting into the notion of risk taking. We must give ourselves permission to take a risk and to believe — really believe — that we can pull it off...that it is the right thing for us to be doing at this time.

In his book *Risking*, Dr. David Viscott emphasizes that success falls more to the courageous, to those with the "will to leap."[1] Supporting this thesis is Muriel James who, in her book *Breaking Free*, gives us a wonderful definition of will — "The determination to act in spite of self-doubt."[2] The process of maturity, as James suggests, is really a process of breaking free. We are all born into a certain amount of mental and emotional bondage that we need to overcome.

It is this very act of personal liberation that Martin Luther had in mind when he likened our lives on earth to a personal passage through the Red Sea. But, we have to buy the ticket, we have to take away the stone. The old adage, "Many are called but few are chosen" might more appropriately be altered to read, "Many are called but few get up from their rocking chairs." Let's not let that be true of us.

Dr. Viscott suggests the best way to get in touch with yourself is to seek a high goal with all your energy. Viscott observes "when you have a goal worth risking for, your actions become purposeful and your life begins to make sense...and then no risk can hold you back."[3] Viscott cautions that "the final push is a 'lonely act,' for no one can know or understand what you are 'becoming' but yourself."[4] No one can monitor your needle readings or issue you the "iasm" passkey but yourself. As was mentioned earlier, you're the only one wired to your applause meter.

The ultimate and most discerning source of permission will never be anyone other than yourself. This is not to say we shouldn't seek or accept outside counsel. It merely cautions that the final arbiter has to be you.

A good therapist can skillfully guide you back inside yourself and help you confront what needs to be confronted. Counselors play a significant role facilitating this confrontation process. But, they overstep their boundaries if they attempt to impart direction and meaning for you.

The key decisions in life are not meant to be consensus decisions. It's okay to seek advice provided you weigh the opinions appropriately, with your own opinion receiving the heaviest weight. This is one arena where you have to learn to throw your weight around. It's not only desirable, it's mandatory.

Someone once said life is really a handful of key decisions surrounded by a plethora of minor ones. You can invest as many of the minor ones as you want in choices that please others and perhaps enhance the moment by doing so.   But to go against your own needle readings on critical choices such as college major, career, mate, home and key friendships is to plant a seed of detachment that will rob you of the "iasm" passkey and block you from riding a wave of energy and fulfillment throughout your life.

Permission stands at the center of the storm — the linchpin of the breaking-free process.   Your applause meter is your built-in compass, marking the way to permission's inner sanctuary.   A strong needle reading, indicating strong inner desire and conviction, can buoy you despite the absence of authorizing ceremony and formal credentials.   But the latter can never make up for an unresponsive needle; for a lack of passion and desire.   There's a decided current in each of your rivers.   Life is learning to locate and accept your current, then operating within it, not against it; learning to go with the flow...your flow.

Permission is not easily gained.   It is a gift you give yourself and you acquire it by first "listening in," and then committing to pursue activities in keeping with the magnitude of your needle readings.   I'm not suggesting a life of indulgence, anarchy and narcissism — far from it.   This is not a "if it feels good then do it" elixir.   What I am suggesting is that you resist the pressure to please others when confronted with life's milestone decisions.   Shakespeare had it right years ago when he wrote, "To thine own self be true."

Don't mistake this for egocentrism.   It is not an outgrowth of the Me Generation and me-first movements.   It is, however, a formula for going undefeated in life and for putting yourself first, not out of a motive of selfishness and aloofness, but for reasons of personal growth and fulfillment. It is a formula for advancing yourself to a level of contentment and peace of mind so that all your relationships and involvements become strengthened and enhanced.   The energy and exuberance so released will reverberate through your very being, re-enforcing your own resolve and serving as a beacon of encouragement within your family, friends and sphere of influence.   The beneficial effects are addictive and will radiate still further to all of society. Walter Truett Anderson recognized this ripple effect when he observed in his book *The Upstart Spring*, "Perhaps there's something political in the human potential movement. Perhaps the humane society the civil rights activists and peace protesters seek is to be reached by a long march through the psyche, through countless acts of personal transformation."[5] Your One-Minute P.E.P. Talk is designed to help you achieve just such a personal transformation...the one about to begin momentarily.

You've probably begun to sense the convergence of a number of earlier topics around this notion of permission. The life of adventure Helen Keller spoke of is within reach once we heed our own needle readings and re-order our life accordingly; once we make what Robert Fritz calls a structural shift from the reactive/responsive orientation to the creative orientation. This is what Fritz calls a "fundamental choice," deciding to pursue a creative vision based on inner desire, not external circumstance(s).[6] The attainment of this structural shift in our lives is what Martin Buber, the late Jewish philosopher, called "taking our stand." It is what Martin Luther, the father of the reformation, likened to a personal passage through the Red Sea.

Whatever your circumstance and reason for undertaking this program, it's a time of freedom, release and new-found energy; a time for reflection, commitment and new beginnings. As Robert Bly, the American poet and modern-day troubadour would say, "It's time to get the doorknob on your side of the door."[7]

It's also time to assemble your commercial.

NOTES:
[1] Dr. David Viscott, *Risking*, (New York: Simon & Schuster, 1977), p. 17.
[2] Muriel James, *Breaking Free*, (Los Angeles: Noah Publishing, 1971), p. 48.
[3] Viscott, *Risking*. p. 15.
[4] Ibid, p. 207.
[5] Walter Truett Anderson, *The Upstart Spring*, (Menlo Park, Ca.: Addison-Wesley, 1983), p. 291.
[6] Robert Fritz, *The Path of Least Resistance*, (New York: Fawcett Columbine, 1989), p. 187.
[7] Robert Bly, *Iron John*, (New York: Addison-Wesley Publishing Co., 1990), p. 178.

Chapter 7

CREATING YOUR OWN ONE-MINUTE P.E.P. TALK

This is where the rubber meets the road; where the rhetoric is put aside and the actual program begins; where you begin to identify and document what you deeply desire to become and emulate in your life, and the beliefs and attitudes you want to guide and shape your thoughts and actions in the future.

On the next few pages are a number of unfinished goal statements in the form of 3" X 5" index cards. What I'd like you to do is grab a pencil and begin to fill in the blanks. If you've already read *The Me Encounter* your cards are essentially done. If this is your first pass at the exercise, the sample cards provided in the Appendix (page 117) will give you a sense of what's required.

Editor's Note: You may find it helpful to get your thoughts down on paper first and then edit them over to the suggested index cards. You'll need a pencil, some paper and five 3" X 5" index cards to complete this exercise. Good luck and take your time. If after due deliberation you find the information is not forthcoming, the author suggests, as a next step, you

> consider reading *The Me Encounter*, the
> section dealing with self-discovery and self-
> renewal beginning on page 119. Resolve
> first where you want to go before involving
> yourself with how to get there — the
> domain of *The Strength to Strive*.

The intent of the cards is to force you to capture on paper what you believe in, stand for and wish to become. The exercise will automatically bring to a head and prompt a host of decisions and prioritization on what is and what is not important to you. The sheer act of writing it down will help you dissipate any directional logjams of old, sharpening your focus and strengthening your resolve in the process.

Let's begin with a list of your beliefs. The intent here, as with the balance of the exercise, is not to impress any would-be reader of your thoughts, but to capture what makes you the special person that you are and intend to become. You will begin to isolate the attributes and the characteristics that you wish to strengthen in yourself and the personal goals that you are now prepared to officially embrace.

The first card, then, should contain a list of all the things you feel strongly about. If the list spills over onto the back of the card, that's fine. We'll tighten down on the list later.

Please develop your list now, using the following format (remember to refer to the Appendix if you get stuck):

MY BELIEFS

I believe ....in_____

...in _____

...in _____

...in _____

...in _____

...in _____

...in _____

...in _____

...in _____

...in _____

Taking the time to reconfirm what you value and hold in high esteem should serve as an excellent warmup for identifying your primary goals.

Please do so now in the space provided below:

MY GOALS

Overall... _____

_____

Family... _____

Career... _____

Mental... _____

Physical... _____

Social.... _____

Community... _____

Spiritual... _____

With your goals fresh in mind, let's ensure your priorities match up with your time allocations. One way to do this — and I apologize for any discomfort this may cause — is to pretend you have just been informed you have only six months to live. As part of the same scenario, accept for the moment that your financial and legal affairs are in order. The question is, how would you spend your last six months on earth? Which of the above goals would you emphasize? Now, please place an asterisk next to the goal or goals you would be inclined to emphasize.

At this point in the exercise, you should have a pretty good idea of the types of behavior and attributes you want to either add or subtract from your day-to-day activities. You should be able to identify the things you want to practice each day to improve upon. I call these aspirations your "be-attitudes" and room is provided below for you to record them. Please do so now. Remember to refer to the Appendix if you get stuck or need a few examples.

MY "BE-ATTITUDES"

To try harder to...
...be more_____
...be less _____
...be more _____
...be less _____
...be a better _____
...be a better _____
...be more _____
...be _____
...be _____

The purpose of the remaining two cards is to begin to tie this exercise together and to state in a positive way what it is you most desire to become and where you plan to place your emphasis. Having done this, the final card will tend to write itself as you zero in on the key action steps that will lead to your most important goals.

Please complete those final cards now:

I AM IN THE PROCESS OF BECOMING...

... _____
... _____
... _____
... _____
... _____
... _____

THEREFORE, REMEMBER TO...

... _____

... _____

... _____

... _____

... _____

... _____

◆ ◆ ◆

Congratulations. The difficult part of assembling your sixty-second commercial — the script — is done. It's "in the can" as they say in the world of broadcast production. And thanks to the movie theater in your mind, the visuals will be arresting, poignant and detail-laced.

Using a technique referred to as a "guided visualization," your assignment, in a moment, will be to picture yourself at the precise instant your most treasured goal is realized. Whether that goal is a career, sports, or academic or social achievement, you'll be pushing on the visual to prop and stage it as close to reality as your imagination will allow, to include background and foreground noise, etc. You'll scan the scene in your mind's eye the way you might in real life, staying with it until you see and feel a release and experience a surge of feelings — the same winning feelings that would buoy and energize you on the actual occasion.

Once those marvelous, uplifting feelings are triggered and the visual begins to fade, you hear a voice — perhaps your own — narrating the contents of the last two cards, proclaiming what you are in the process of becoming and what you are remembering to do. The key is to express them as present-tense facts, not hopes for the future.

As the voice trails off, treat yourself again to a repeat of the key visual, picturing yourself attaining your goal and, if appropriate, being recognized for the achievement. If there are accolades involved, stay with the visual until you hear, see and feel the applause. See yourself acknowledging and responding to the recognition. Most importantly, zero in on how good you feel about yourself. Embrace the feeling like you would a long-lost friend. Experience the unbounded energy that accompanies such moments and pull as much as you can back into the present as you prepare to release the visual.

After you've done this once or twice you'll probably find your commercial taking on a life of its own. Some days the visual will be easy to bring forth and you'll be pleasantly surprised at the ancillary details that suddenly fill the screen. The quality and forcefulness of the narration will likely also vary, but the effect on your subconscious will be powerful and additive. Even on the days and the occasions when the visual is elusive and remote, don't give up on it. The words will carry the day and another valuable repetition will be registered and recorded within your subconscious, opening yet wider the space in your life for those envisioned events to eventually happen.

SOME EXAMPLES

Any new undertaking can be daunting at first. A few examples are offered here to ease any lingering doubts; to help you muster the will and the determination to begin by showing how the one-minute P.E.P. Talk tool can work in everyday life.

One example from each goal category is offered (i.e. career, spouse, social, mental, physical fitness, community) to substantiate the tool's versatility. Read through them with an eye toward grasping the underlying technique, not necessarily the arbitrarily selected content. The range of possible scenarios is endless, limited only by your innermost desire and your imagination.

Your applause meter will sort out which category and which goal warrant your initial focus. Bear in mind, you're simply putting structure around a replacement thought and a replacement visual, essentially indulging in some good, old-fashioned daydreaming — daydreaming that's guided by a preselected goal and seeded with supportive, positive affirmations. Like climbing back on a bicycle after years away, your daydreaming skills should return effortlessly. No doubt you've been using them all along.

Creating your one-minute commercial is the easy part. If there's a challenge to be met, it will be in the area of implementation — remembering to implement your commercial during the early days before your new resolve has had time to acquire the force of habit. It's here you'll need to channel your attention and focus your will. Once again, "well begun is half done."

The commercial is nothing more than an organized daydream. Unlike some daydreams however, it won't be wandering off into the realm of fantasy and groundless aspiration. It will target an important, achievable goal that you and you alone decide is within reach and essential to your continued growth.

Earlier we likened the act of setting and visualizing your goal, a milestone event unto itself, as comparable to dropping a log on the bank at a river's bend. Each subsequent repetition of your commercial has the effect of dropping yet another mental log on that metaphoric river bank, forever altering the topography of the bank and your life in the process, and providing you with the propulsion to keep your self-doubt in check long enough to stay the course. All the while, you will be buttressed by a growing and deeply rooted belief that you can and will bring the envisioned event to fruition.

As evidence accumulates that your efforts are beginning to have the desired effect on your life, the process is reenforced and your energy and conviction will strengthen further. You'll be on your way to recreating your life according to a script you've chosen, propelled by an energy that emanates from the very core of your being.

Let's look at a few examples. In each case, the visual is detail-laced in an effort to make it as realistic as possible so your subconscious accepts the experience as reality.

Example #1 (Career)

Situation: Your job often requires that you speak to groups varying in size. You have never been comfortable as a public speaker. You fear your nervousness shows and will interfere with your effectiveness and future career advancement.

Goal:

You'd like to greet each audience with a relaxed smile and a confident manner, focusing your thoughts on the group, the occasion and your message, not on yourself and your nervousness.

One-Minute
Commercial:

Visual — The scene opens with you sitting quietly amidst a group of business associates. The annual sales meeting is underway. You've fretted over this meeting in the past, but on this occasion you're prepared and confident. You can tell from the sporadic coughing and movement within the audience the speaker at the podium is not going over well. It wasn't too long ago that such a sight might have triggered the release of a squadron of butterflies, but today is different. You see yourself sitting poised and collected as the speaker concludes his remarks and turns the podium over to you.

Having seconds before previewed this moment in your mind's eye (using your one-minute P.E.P. Talk) you watch as you now confidently rise and approach the front. You look calm and not the least bit nervous, despite the audience's evident impatience and subdued mumbling. You watch as you make eye contact with the previous speaker and a few associates seated near the front.

A relaxed smile emerges on your face as you acknowledge the introduction, the occasion and a key point from the previous talk. As you do so, you hear the service personnel preparing the refreshments in the back for the break that follows your address. Undeterred, you move into your material in a relaxed and deliberate manner. Your opening remarks go smoothly. You've got the group's attention and begin to feel a boost of energy and renewed confidence. Your whole demeanor is proclaiming "I'm relaxed, prepared and in control."

The words and gestures are flowing on cue. As you get to your closing statement, your rhythm and delivery has never been better. The impact is compelling and poignant. The audience is 100% absorbed. Even the sound of a passing siren doesn't intrude on your wrap up. You thank them for their attention, smiling warmly. You pause to accept and acknowledge their spirited applause, then ask them to join you for refreshments at the rear tables. As you collect your notes and spot check your watch, you graciously accept congratulatory comments from those you pass as you make your way through the room. A supportive wink from your boss adds to your growing exuberance.

Narration — Just before you descend the podium, as you watch yourself basking in the spontaneous applause, the voice-over intrusively declares: "A poised, relaxed public speaker...begins with a confident air, keeps the talk interesting and well-paced, and closes with a flourish...a real professional!"

Visual — As the voice-over concludes, you once again see, in flashback sequence, yourself confidently approaching the podium. You zoom in as you flash that quick, ready smile and enjoy again the concluding round of applause. You allow the noise of the applause to build as you bask in the glow of the moment. Continuing to savor the exuberant feeling now swelling within you, the narrator's closing words are heard again..."a real professional!"

You watch as you make your way through the admiring crowd and you vow to freeze frame this moment, deciding to capture it for future insertion into your consciousness — to prime the pump — the next time you're called upon to speak.

Example #2 (Spouse)

Situation:

Like most marriages, yours has had its ups and downs. After nine years together, you've begun to take each other for granted. The greetings are no longer affectionate and the goodbyes are businesslike and flat. You realize you've invested considerable time attending to your career but have allowed your marriage to somehow take care of itself. You've seen too many marriages atrophy and break apart and yours could be next if you don't take action now.

Goal:

You'd like to recapture some of the sparkle and the tenderness that filled your courtship and early relationship. You made each other feel special then and being together was joyful in itself. You decide to improve your "I'm home" greeting in the future. To convey with your eyes, words, actions and tone that this is your favorite time of day...that going to work is an important part of who you are but coming home is where you get your sustenance and emotional zest.

One-Minute
Commercial:

Visual — The scene opens with you arriving home, about to put the key in the door. The sight of the key triggers you to recall that the "key" to a happier, more intimate atmosphere at home is the opening ten seconds. Rather than quietly entering and going straight to the mail, you enter with a smile and a purposeful spring to your step. You're happy to be home and your whole being communicates that fact. You watch as you kick off your shoes and greet the family pet. You follow up your announcement "Honey, I'm home" by heading off in the direction of the reply. You meet in the hallway. Warm eye contact is followed by a hug and a heartfelt kiss. You disregard the pile of mail for the moment and ask about your spouse's day. You listen intently despite the sudden ringing of the telephone. You affirm your interest with another hug before reaching for the telephone. You watch as you divide your attention between the phone caller and your pet who has reappeared at your feet looking for additional stroking.

Narration — As your welcome-home hug is in full embrace, a voice-over announces: "Jobs may come and go but your love for (spouse) will endure forever. You lost touch with this closeness for awhile but it won't happen again. Your life is full and all is well in your world."

Visual — As the narrator's voice fades, you see a flashback of the entire homecoming sequence. From the key ritual at the door to the undying devotion of the family pet, you see it all again as a series of quick cuts. You zoom in on your evident enthusiasm and your spouse's for this reenactment of yester-year brought forth today. You feel a rush of tender feelings as you observe again the hall-way embrace. You feel encouraged and your resolve to continue these greetings is rein-forced as the narrator's concluding words are reprised..."and all is well in your world."

Example #3 (Social)

Situation:

Your social life brings you into contact with dozens of new people. You enjoy these meetings but are embarrassed by your inabil-ity to remember names. On such occasions you believe if you could tune out the distrac-tions and focus solely on each new name you would improve your recall measurably. You believe the problem is the distracting chatter in your mind. You sense a simple mind game — a preset mental image — could help you capture and set each name in your memory. An image that would force you to stop and focus your attention on each name as it is voiced.

Goal:

To condition your mind to invoke this mind game each and every time you make a new acquaintance, thereby forcing yourself to cap-ture each name and repeat it out loud as you establish and hold eye contact.

One-Minute
Commercial:

Visual — The scene opens on a large gather-ing at a nearby hotel. You're attending an event for a local charity and are standing in a small group. A couple you've known for years approaches with a new couple. After exchanging greetings, the moment you've been conditioning yourself for arrives. The distractions are many. Everyone is dressed to the hilt and it's hard to stay focused. The trays of hors d'oeuvres circulating through the room are a tasty distraction as well. In the midst of all this, your friend motions to you and says "I'd like you to meet the Booths, Rita and Howard." To complicate matters, just as their names are given the group next to you erupts in laughter. But faithful to your new resolve and as if on cue, you see yourself block out the distractions as you capture in your mind's eye their names in a clear plastic box which snaps closed around them. The box appears as if superimposed in the upper left corner on the visual you're picturing. The names are glowing and readable from without. You watch as you make eye contact and greet each of the Booths by name. To help set the last name in your mind you ask if Booth is spelled with or without an e at the end. They reply "without an e" and seem genuinely pleased with the attention you're extending to their name. Your favorite hors d'oeuvre passed by in the process but you've got hold of something more important. When your friends resume circulating through the crowd, you'll be able to address the Booths by name as you express pleasure on having met.

Narrative — The voice-over message is simple and employs a memory-assisting mnemonic device — an imaginary plastic box that "snaps" shut around each elusive name. As your friends and the new couple approach, the voice-over intrusively interrupts: "Remembering their name will be a 'SNAP.' Hear it. Picture it. 'SNAP' it. You'll own it. It's a snap...'SNAP.'

Visual — As the voice-over concludes, the visual returns to the precise moment you first hear the Booth's name spoken. The camera zooms in on the imaginary plastic box as the lid 'SNAPS' shut and the names illuminate within:

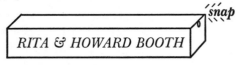

RITA & HOWARD BOOTH

The camera lingers on the box as you hear yourself recognize the Booths by name as they depart. As you enjoy the feeling of accomplishment, your spouse shoots you an approving glance. You whisper, "It was a snap. Rita and Howard Booth without an 'e'... SNAP."

Example #4 (Mental)

Situation: You've just about finished reading *The Strength to Strive*. You're struck by the premise that you need to be ever mindful of where you let your prevalent thoughts go, that there is a casual relationship between your thoughts, your conversations, your resultant expectations and what you subsequently experience in life. Guided by the book's central message that "the action starts in your mind," you decide to begin seeding your thoughts and commit to do it for at least twenty-one days before assessing the results. As suggested, you decide to look for the GOOD in each and every moment — to give people the benefit of the doubt. You believe the majority of people are doing the best they can even though their behavior and remarks might suggest otherwise.

Goal:

You want to recondition your mind to be less prone to critically interpret the intent and the behavior of others. You've heard that within many adults is a young, struggling child who may not have had all of his or her developmental needs met. You want to honor this by remembering to substitute a replacement thought the next time you feel compelled to react angrily or to judge another harshly. You believe by pausing for a moment to picture and embrace your own inner child (i.e. yourself at age six, eight or ten), you'll be enabled and empowered to then say to yourself "They're doing the best they can right now."

One-Minute
Commercial:

Visual — The scene opens with you sitting in your car in a line of traffic. Two lanes are converging into one and the alternate merge is going smoothly until the car that is supposed to defer to you doesn't let you in. As you feel your blood pressure rise and your grip on the steering wheel tighten, you're inclined to blow your horn and express your displeasure. After mentally finding the culprit bereft of any redeeming attributes (all in the span of two to three seconds) you regain your composure. You catch a glimpse of your own inner child and sit back in your seat as you visualize the inner child likely at the wheel in the car ahead. You're glad you didn't overreact, and feel a growing pride in your new-found control.

Narrative — You're milliseconds away from making a scene when the voice-over intrudes into your consciousness: "Whoa...either his inner child is at the wheel or he's daydreaming. Either way, relax, he's doing the best he can...and so are you."

Visual — As the voice-over fades, you catch another glimpse of your own inner child and the tension recedes further. The voice-over returns: "Whoa ... remember, he's doing the best he can."

Example #5 (Physical Fitness)

Situation:

For years you've watched as more and more of your friends have joined health clubs and taken responsibility for their health and well-being. After years of telling yourself "one of these days," your doctor has given you the incentive you lacked before. He wants you to lose ten pounds and begin to exercise to keep your circulation from deteriorating further. At your doctor's suggestion, you've joined the local "Y" and enrolled in an aerobics class.

You've never been much for regimented exercise and are concerned whether you can muster the resolve to attend all fifteen of the twice-weekly classes. You decide this is the perfect time to implement the one-minute P.E.P. Talk program.

Goal:

Since this represents a major change, you sense you need to begin at the beginning — like remembering to pack your gym bag Monday and Wednesday evenings so you're equipped on Tuesdays and Thursdays to attend the 6 PM sessions straight from work. You decide to remind yourself to pack as part of your retiring routine. You also decide to picture yourself fitting right in and getting into the flow of the program early on.

One-Minute
Commercial:

Visual — The scene opens with you in your bedclothes moments before retiring. As you reach out to switch on the alarm you notice the reminder card and its "GYM BAG" message. On the floor next to your bedside table, you open the bag to see if it contains a clean outfit and your sneakers. You place it alongside your briefcase so you won't overlook it when you dash off to work in the morning.

The scene then jumps ahead to 6:15 PM the following day. You see yourself in your aerobics class dutifully following the lead of your instructor. You're pleased to see a good mix of men and women and few look even remotely close to winning any body-beautiful awards. Happily, you're not struggling to keep up and are actually having a good time. When you do fall behind, you just pause for a second and soon you're back in step. The beat of the music is easy to follow — almost exhilarating — and the colorful array of gym outfits gyrating around you adds to your enjoyment. You can see the relief on your face. You're not sticking out as you had feared.

Narration — After witnessing your relief at fitting in easily, the visual returns to the night-before ritual and in quick-cut sequence, you fast forward to the 6:15 PM session itself. You hear your conscience in the form of a voice-over declare, "You're organized, you're involved and you fit in." The visual moves along until you're back to enjoying the music and the colorful outfits. At that point, the visual freeze-frames on you and your voice-over conscience softly declares..."and to think I was afraid I wouldn't fit in."

Visual — As the action resumes, it's as if someone turned the music volume up and everyone's enthusiasm level similarly rises. You focus in on your own elevated mood as you hear yourself chuckle "and to think I was afraid I wouldn't fit in."

Example #6 (Community, Environment, Health)

Situation: You've smoked for years and the time has come to give it up once and for all. You've tried, on occasion, in the past but never could sustain your resolve. This time is different. This time you're committed to do it. No more self-praise just for "trying."

Goal: To condition yourself to trigger in your mind's eye, a vivid one-minute commercial at the first inkling of a nicotine craving. In essence, to fight the craving with a poignant visual and a sobering narrative that dramatically portray where you're headed if you succumb and give in to the craving. In essence, get yourself to dwell — really dwell — on the consequences of not stopping. The pictures you'll be creating are not pleasant, but neither is the fate you're trying to avoid.

One-Minute
Commercial:

Visual — The scene opens with an aerial shot high above a cemetery. A burial is just concluding as the camera zooms in on the crowd, then on the headstone. The shock of seeing your family assembled is jolting. As the camera isolates on the headstone and it's your name that's inscribed — with a date that's uncomfortably close to the present — you let out a gasp.

Narrative — With the camera locked on the headstone, you begin to hear some familiar voices. It's your family and their sadness is magnified because this could have been avoided. Between sobs, you hear, "Why couldn't _____ see this coming. Why didn't he/she stop. It's so senseless, so tragically needless. Maybe if he/she could have glimpsed this moment, and felt our pain, things could have been different."

Visual — As the camera pulls back from the headstone, the family has left and a worker is patting the sod in place. Perspiring and ready for a break, the worker reaches into his pocket for a cigarette but stops abruptly as you and he both relive your families pain..." Maybe if _____ could have glimpsed this moment, things could have been different." The scene then goes black.

This is a good spot to pause and review what we've covered to this point as a primer to our discussion of why it will work for you once implemented. The Dolphin team of 1972 was highlighted to register a number of key points. Implicit in their example is the assumption that the same operative dynamics that propelled and empowered their success in 1972 can be brought to bear on your life as well.

We saw that the Dolphins' success traced to two fundamentals: their "power of belief" and "level of preparedness." Their secret weapon — Don Shula — never logged a minute of game time yet he influenced every second of every game. He did it through the strength of his character and his powerful presence; a presence that was steadfastly there through endless hours of practice and discussion. Shula's full-court press involvement provided a daily and hourly infusion of energy and conviction. For those not naturally gifted with such inner belief and resolve, they could hitchhike on Coach Shula's energy and enthusiasm, gradually adding to their own in the process.

What training camp amounted to was total immersion and exposure to a system and a philosophy that progressively squeezed failure out of the players' active vocabulary. In time, they grew in their knowledge, skills, conditioning and teamwork. And underneath it all, untracked and unreported, the players grew in the most powerful way of all. They grew in their "belief" in themselves, in the team, and in the organization. Their hard work, discipline and commitment had vaulted them past that uncharted threshold point where belief, once released and nurtured, is itself mysteriously transformed into conviction; where your belief is so total that you actually expect to prevail in the end; where your self-doubt demons are banished and you find yourself walking a little taller, feeling confident and secure that you are prepared and ready.

The mortar that kept the Dolphins' wall of conviction in tact was Don Shula himself. A quick glimpse of his imposing presence on the sideline could trigger a positive surge — the same sort of positive surge your one-minute commercial will now pull from you on demand in the future. The same boost I experienced quite by chance some twenty years ago from that inspirational plaque in Coach Shula's office.

Make no mistake about it. Replacement thoughts work, and they work big time when fortified and braced with supporting visuals that go to work on your sub-conscious and your very be-ing, giving you permission to believe and permission to put forth a full-court press — the full-court press that will be needed to sustain you in your quest, insuring the "iasm" pass-key remains in your possession.

The key link in the chain comes early. Search your heart and accumulated life experience to identify the playing field where you choose to make your stand; where you feel intrin-sically most comfortable and where the fit feels right; where the "iasm" passkey seems close enough to grasp if not already firmly planted in your pocket; where the hard work ahead will not be hard work at all, but a labor of love; and where the sheer pur-suit of your goal quickens your step and beckons you onward.

Paul Kurtz was on the mark when he wrote "it is in the pro-cess of attainment that we thrive." What needs to be empha-sized, however, is that this dynamic only applies to goals that you actively and passionately choose for yourself. Goals and involvements of the rocking-chair variety are fatally flawed at their inception, with the seeds of their ultimate demise likely heralded by the subjects unresponsive applause meter.

What makes me so confident that what I'm espousing here works? In addition to the story of the plaque depicted earlier — evidence of the impact a replacement thought can have on our feelings and behavior — I've got the best possible proof to offer. In fact, you're holding it right now. This very book is proof positive the One-Minute P.E.P. Talk regimen can change your life.

Before you dismiss this as just another puff of self-serving smoke, there's an important fact you need to know. At this very moment — Monday, May 13, 1991; 4:03 P.M. EST — *The Strength to Strive* is just a proposed title, a personal dream and the second of two books I've decided to write without the slight-est inkling or assurance the public would be even interested much less motivated to buy and read them. Months and per-haps years will pass before *The Strength to Strive* begins to attain whatever recognition and acclaim will ultimately lead you to pick it up. This may seem academic, but the point is simply this — whatever success awaits me as a writer and a speaker, it hasn't happened yet!

We are much closer in our respective life journeys than you might think. Yes, I've committed to making a career change — the proverbial "leap" if you will — but I'm still in midair. At the time of this writing, I have yet to land a publisher for my first literary effort *The Me Encounter*, my last paycheck was longer ago than I care to remember and many of my acquaintances are questioning my sanity, to say nothing of my judgment.

In actuality, I'm only a few chapters ahead of you. If these words are actually coming to you in book form, that's great news for both of us. The regimen works!

Chapter 8 ——————

SYNAPTIC EFFICACY & CHANGE

Since time immemorial, the human spirit has wrestled with this thing we call the "human condition." Volumes have been written and entire lives dedicated to the pursuit of answers and a definitive road map.

The mere mention of the subject still sparks debate after centuries of exploration. Voices from the philosophy, theology, psychology and medical fields are frequent participants. More faddish and cult-type voices have emerged and receded over the years, offering a parade of ultimate answers and solutions. Yet the quest persists.

All the while, as our greatest minds and thinkers grappled with the issue on a macro level, for mankind in general, legends of individuals conducted their own ad hoc inquisitions in the quiet and often lonely caverns of their individual minds and psyches. The struggle has far from abated.

Sigmund Freud identified what he called the "compulsion to repetition" which seems to propel each of us to continually repeat previous behavior, approaching what a computer programmer might call a closed-loop program. We'll spend some time in this chapter describing and understanding the force that causes this to happen. In the process, we'll discover we can exert far more control over our lives than we're probably now aware...that, in fact, we've been influencing it all along.

What will be made increasingly clear is that becoming a happier, more fulfilled person is really an "inside" job...and **THE ACTION BEGINS IN YOUR MIND.** The same natural forces that pull you down and lock you into habitual negative thoughts and behavior patterns can be redirected to free you from the tyranny of the past, free to rechannel your life into a future of your own choosing.

As you grow in your understanding of why you tend to act and react the way you do, you will also grow in your resolve to stay the course here. This resolve and propulsion begins to flow from the enlightened belief that the One-Minute P.E.P. Talk regimen works, both in theory and in practice.

The answer is to be found in a deeper understanding of how our mind operates; how our thoughts and feelings get recorded, are subsequently triggered, and then brought back into the present. What we're about to discuss and chart may well validate Freud's "compulsion to repetition" theory. A word of caution, however. Before you conclude we're condemned by this dynamic to forever repeat the past — a past we had virtually no control over — we'll invoke Newton's Third Law to obviate such a fatalistic and erroneous conclusion.

Unlike lower animal forms born with innate instincts to guide their day-to-day existence, we humans are not similarly preprogrammed. On the contrary, we are complex learning machines born with a vast yet empty memory bank. We begin with a clean slate, if you will, that we spend a lifetime only partially filling up. What we often fail to realize is just how pervasive our early learning is and how the process is meant to continue throughout life if we don't impede it.

Benjamin Disraeli, leader of the Conservative Party in 1860s England, once observed, "As a rule...he or she who has the most information will have the most success in life."[1] But human learning is not limited to collecting facts in school. Actually, by the time we reach school we've recorded a vast amount of information, much of which forms the foundation of our future "inner life" (i.e., our feelings, emotional balance, automatic thoughts and in general our outlook on life and our sense of self and self-esteem).

Let's take a moment for a brief introduction to what is called Transactional Analysis (T.A.). Don't be put off by the fancy title. It's really quite simple. In the process, what we'll acquire is a heightened awareness and appreciation for how the infant and child mind acts as a sponge, absorbing and recording everything it encounters. We'll also acquire a new vocabulary that will help us track and call forth some key new concepts. Should this section serve to whet your appetite to learn more about T.A., I direct you to Dr. Thomas A. Harris' classic, *I'm OK -- You're OK*, a book which richly lives up to its subtitle "A Practical Guide to Transactional Analysis."

What Dr. Harris correctly saw in T.A. was a teaching and learning device that, while particularly relevant for group therapy, was instructive on the conversational level also. It avoided what he found much individual therapy to be: namely, "a confessional or an archeological exploration of the psychic cellars."[2]

T.A. simply views life as a series of events or transactions, each of which we sequentially experience. We observe, interpret and respond to each. The discipline distinguishes three states of being or entities in each person's make-up: the Parent, the Child, and the Adult.

We'll get into each of the three states of being in a moment, but for now it might be helpful to think of them as three separate tape recordings. At any given moment, in response to any given transactional stimulus or event, one of those tapes will be selected and played as a response. The Parent and Child tapes, since they were recorded first, are held to be on primary circuits, literally hard-wired into our consciousness. The Adult tape comes later, if we're lucky. Its very presence and share of "air time" in our consciousness, can be directly correlated with our level of maturity and personal freedom.

From the moment of our birth and throughout our childhood, we are busy "recording." Both external and internal events are monitored and captured. The external events are largely interactions with our parents, wherein we capture all the "do not's" and a few "do's" from their continuous stream of instructions and injunctions. This tape is the "taught" concept of life and is labeled our "Parent."

The internal events are also all recorded, but are of a different sort. They have to do with the feelings we experienced as infants and toddlers, the responses of that little person to all that was seen and heard. This tape is the "felt" concept of life and is labeled our "Child."

By the time we reach the age of reason, our Parent and Child tapes are already quite extensive, and we had no conscious choice in the matter. It seems unfair, yet nonetheless true, that this early parental inheritance that can so profoundly influence the rest of our days, is <u>initially</u> out of our control. I underscore initially because that's where the "Adult" state-of-being comes into play.

While the Adult state begins early in life, (some feel about the time a baby attains mobility), it also has a subordinate, tentative position for quite some time. The function and role of the Adult is to gradually sort through the old Parent and Child tapes and to remove those that don't square with observed reality. Since the Parent and Child tapes are on primary circuits, the emerging Adult is easily displaced by its preexisting, formidable foes. Even if the Parent tape is not invoked, any number of things can happen to us that recreate situations of early childhood, thereby triggering the feelings we felt back then. When this happens, the Child tape often takes over. When a person is pulled back to these early, infantile feelings, it is said that the event has "hooked their Child." The behavior that ensues is — you guessed it — downright childish.

A good analogy is to view the Adult as a screening computer. A computer which, as the person grows and matures, gains strength and air time for its growing inventory of accepted, empirically verified Parent and Child recordings.

I find it helpful to liken the ongoing conversation we conduct with ourselves, in the confines of our mind, as akin to the play-by-play commentary during a sports broadcast. Like at a game, the commentary is nonstop. The only thing in question at any point in time is which of our three states of being has command of the microphone or "mike." Said differently, which is getting the most air time in our lives?

To the extent the Adult is able to elbow its way in and wrest control of the "mike," the person is said to have gained maturity. The presence of a strong Adult brings the element of choice into play, freeing the person from the constant pull of his or her past.

The goal of T.A. is to encourage the growth and air time of the Adult, restoring to the individual much of the freedom of choice and the freedom to change that may have been lost in early childhood. This book is similarly intended to restore your freedom and your ability to change, and not to simply illuminate the process but to empower and facilitate it with a good, old-fashioned jump-start push ... a twenty-one-day jump-start push.

A central tenant of T.A., as expressed by Dr. Harris, is that there are four distinct viewpoints of the world. The first three are emotion-driven and the fourth is a rational, thoughtful selection. They are:

1)   I'm Not OK — You're OK

2)   I'm Not OK — You're Not OK

3)   I'm OK — You're Not OK

4)   I'm OK — You're OK[3]

These viewpoints are often referred to as "scripts." Very early in life we are compelled by our emerging feelings to select one of the first three as our script. While it may not be a conscious choice, it is made just the same. The decision is based on the prevalence of stroking in our lives to that point. Dr. Harris feels we all are born into some feelings of "I'm not OK," a natural result of the frustrating, civilizing process as we pass from infancy into early childhood. A word of caution — be careful not to affix blame. It is the situation of childhood and not the intent of the parents that produces the problem. Any actual neglect on the parents part will only magnify the "not OK" feelings.

Importantly, once we establish this central emotional position, it becomes the position we gravitate to for the rest of our lives, unless we consciously choose #4 later. The presence of a strong Adult is what will encourage and empower this hoped-for and highly desirable movement to position #4.

Central to the T.A. doctrine is that all our subsequent experiences are *selectively interpreted* to support our early position. And what is downright insidious about this support phenomenon is that it is not only self-perpetuating, it gains momentum over time. The property of the brain that causes this to happen is something called SYNAPTIC EFFICACY.

Strange as it seems, and as advanced as our medical science is, we're only now beginning to understand how the brain controls the body. The brain is not only the center of thought, it functions as a sort of apothecary dispenser releasing a variety of chemicals and hormone-like substances that can have both subtle and profound effects upon the body.

While much of the brain remains a mystery, we do know we're each born with in excess of ten billion nerve cells, called neurons, at birth. These neurons respond to stimulation and conduct messages, our thoughts included among them. This communication between neurons is chemical, made possible by a range of specialized chemicals called neurotransmitters.

The area where two neurons come close together, the gap that is spanned by the neurotransmitters, is called the "synapse." Current theory holds that when our mind records an event or captures a thought, a linkage is made between selected neurons. The word engram is often used to label each such memory unit.

Synaptic efficacy is a central premise of this emerging new field (see Figures 4-6) which suggests that as a particular engram is called forth into consciousness, the ease of connection between those particular neurons gets easier with use. Likewise, it will weaken through disuse.

One way to understand the concept is to liken it to running a pencil back and forth between two points, in this case two specific neurons, each time we entertain a particular thought. The more frequently we trigger that engram, the darker the pencil line becomes. In time that thought, that engram, will join the ranks of our top-of-mind, most prevalent thoughts. It attains that status because of the air time we have given it. Whether the thought is valid or squares with reality is a different matter.

Synaptic efficacy explains the strength and early persistence of our Parent and Child tapes, earlier described as being on primary circuits. Synaptic efficacy bears out that description by suggesting their respective component engrams were heavily darkened lines, darkened by repeated and early activation, as depicted in Figure 6. Happily, buried in the synaptic efficacy phenomenon and dynamic are the seeds of your ability to change and redirect your future growth. What I'm alluding to is the notion that old engrams will fade with disuse and new ones will gain strength and air time with a concerted effort to darken new lines of your choosing...your core strategy here.

I promised to invoke Newton's Third Law and actually just did. As you may recall from high school science, Newton's Third Law states that a force in motion will tend to stay in motion until acted upon by an outside force. The force in motion to be influenced is your current thought tendencies, and the outside force you will invoke to get the job done is none other than yourself.

You'll be wielding some powerful new tools to ensure the changes you desire not only stick, but root deep. Synaptic efficacy, the culprit and the force behind the echoes from your past, will become your lead friend and ally of the future.

SYNAPTIC EFFICACY

FIG. 4   THE SYNAPSE

    • — — — — — > SYNAPSE <— — — — —•
    NEURON   NEURON

FIG. 5   INFREQUENTLY
                    RECALLED MEMORY/THOUGHT
                            (ENGRAM A)

    •▬▬▬▬▬▬▬▬▬▬▬▬▬▬▬▬▬▬▬▬▬▬
    NEURON   NEURON

FIG. 6   FREQUENTLY
                    RECALLED MEMORY/THOUGHT
                            (ENGRAM B)

    •████████████████████████████
    NEURON   NEURON

NOTES:
[1] Dr. Eric Berne, *Games People Play*, (New York: Grove Press, 1964), p. 29.
[2] Dr. Thomas Harris, *I'm OK — You're OK*, (New York: Harper & Row, 1969), p. xvii.
[3] Ibid. p. 43.

Chapter 9

INTERPRETATIONS & CHOICES

Abraham Lincoln once observed "people are about as happy as they make up their minds to be." There's a word lurking in the background of this seemingly tame statement that many people are not prepared to accept. Yet, emotional freedom and peace of mind will remain forever beyond their grasp until it is acknowledged and heeded.

The word is CHOICE.

Significant advances in medicine, industrial technology and space exploration have dramatically changed the world and life as Lincoln knew it, yet the insightfulness of his words ring as true today as then, perhaps more so. If there's one moment in a person's life that marks the passage of youth into maturity — emotional rather than physical maturity — it would be the moment when we finally realize and *accept* that we each have to create our own world. This is not exactly what many of us want to hear. After years of investing ourselves in blaming others — in reciting chapter and verse why our lives have not fallen into place yet — to even entertain an alternate explanation, much less embrace it, would be too threatening, too much of a self-betrayal.

Paul Kurtz in his book *Exuberance-A Philosophy of Happiness* describes the sobering impact of this unalterable truth as follows: "the destiny of man, of all men and of each man, is that he is condemned to invent what he will be - condemned if he is fearful but blessed if he welcomes the great adventure."[1] The breakthrough occurs when we finally comprehend and accept that what we become in life is our choice...that we already are, in fact, what we have chosen to be so far.

The next few pages are excerpted from *The Me Encounter* chapter on change. They apply equally well here.

◆ ◆ ◆

With only one life to live, it's time to recapture the sense of awe and specialness that surrounded your birth. It's time to begin to live like you really mean it...to get your heart into it.

Figure 7 suggests we are each in pursuit of the same GOOD; we each want to love and be loved and to find a meaningful purpose that will fill our days with energy — born of our accomplishments — and the peace of mind that flows from commitments freely made and earnestly pursued.

Having been made in God's image, man is at his core good. Much like our brethren further down the chart in the animal kingdom, we are biologically preset to mate and raise offspring. We do this in family units and in social groupings where compassion and love hopefully abound. Hopefully, because as Figure 8 suggests, on our way to getting in touch with the GOOD we often encounter obstacles. Due to early childhood experiences, we may have inherited some emotional "not-okay" feelings that will need attention before we can begin to even see the GOOD, much less experience it as a steady diet. The obstacles blocking our path can and do vary widely, yet when reduced to their basics probably are propelled by one or more of the culprit elements listed in Figure 8. Whether readily identifiable as such or dressed up in new clothing, underneath virtually all the obstacles you might enumerate will likely be operating some combination of anger, resentment, misinterpretation and selfishness. The inevitable feelings of disappointment, frustration and deprivation that result, once triggered, can create a barrier and a blockage as strong as any prison wall.

The presence of such obstacles in our lives is more the rule than the exception. In spite of ups and downs, and at times more downs than ups, it does help to remember we have not been singled out for an especially harsh life. The Bible is clear that when Adam and Eve succumbed to temptation, all who followed would, as a consequence, be exposed to good and evil, joy and suffering.

What you're experiencing is what was planned for all of us. The world as we know it was designed to function as a stage. Albert Camus, the French philosopher and author, makes the point that we each need to eventually accept "the benign indifference of the universe." In effect, the stage we are launched upon at birth is just that — a stage. It is a stage we will occupy for an uncertain time, where we will be judged both for the quality of our performance and the script we eventually write for ourselves.

Camus' observation of a "benign indifference" in the universe is a key one — that God propped the stage with equal measures of good and evil. In other words, He set up a fair fight. But make no mistake about it, it was meant to be a fight...a struggle. Martin Luther perhaps said it best when he likened our time on earth to a personal passage through the Red Sea...that we are each put here and challenged to break free from our specific personal inheritance and bondage, much like the Israelites broke free from four hundred years of bondage in Egypt.

An old rabbinical expression states that a man enters life with his fist clenched but leaves with his hand open, suggesting that we each have to progress from holding fast to material possessions to embracing life itself...to investing our thoughts and our time in looking for the GOOD and being creatively alive in the moment.

We discussed in the Introduction there are certain tools we need to help us weather the normal ups and downs of life. As shown in Figure 9, these tools are:

✓ positive self-esteem
✓ positive self-direction
✓ positive attitudes and beliefs

The presence of obstacles in your life (Figure 10) merely indicates you're alive, still on stage and that one or more of these essential tools needs some work. Figure 10 then is designed to show where you likely are right now. The obstacles have accumulated and aggregated over time and block your ability to see or experience much of the GOOD in your life. Figure 11 completes the picture of where you're heading. Through books such as this, *The Me Encounter* and others devoted to obstacle removal or reduction, you'll be opening up numerous new channels or sight lines to help you both see and experience the GOOD on a steady basis.

Your belief system — your attitudes and emotional view of the world — is at the root of all your thoughts, opinions, conversations and actions. It is your on-board computer scanner that drives all your interpretations. You are forever judging and interpreting events around you based on what you believe to be true in the world. The individual programs that instruct and guide this computer scanner are your attitudes. They are that central in your life. If these attitudes and beliefs remain frozen and beyond examination, your growth will stagnate and your life will become truly circular.

What we often fail to realize is how pervasive and dominating our attitudes become. Their hold over us is near tyrannical, and they manifest themselves in our preconceptions and predispositions. They influence how we see and hear the events around us. M. Scott Peck in his wonderful book *The Road Less Traveled* had this to say on the blinding influence of our preconceptions, "Not until our perceptions are disengaged from the domination of our preconceptions are we free to experience the world as it is in itself."[2]

No doubt Socrates had this very thing in mind when he said "The unexamined life is not worth living." He, like Scott Peck, understood that the destroying circularity of a life must be broken by the person living it; that no one else can challenge and remove the attitudes that so control and dictate your behavior. Only you can do this for yourself, and your new one-minute commercial will play a role...a big role.

An awareness of history begins to surface as a key element here. In this case, your own personal history and the unique chain of events that have contributed to who you are at this point in your growth. Kierkegaard had this sorted out years ago when he said "Life can only be understood backwards, but it must be lived forwards." In this context, I believe Kierkegaard was also issuing a caution. Like Socrates, he knew the importance of the backward glance as an aid in understanding and as a perspective enhancer. He also seemed to be warning us not to linger there or to drag the past forward into the present. But that's exactly what we do when we allow the unchallenged attitudes from our past to continue to trigger our thoughts, interpretations and conversations today.

Your attitudes are nothing more than recordings or mental imprints that established an early beachhead in your mind. The more you replayed them, the more entrenched they became and continue to become. Yet, their very existence and the air time they may have usurped in the past in no way implies they were accurate or valid thoughts then or now. They simply got a foothold in your mind before you had any conscious say in the matter. Things are different now. You are awakening to new choices. You need not remain captive to the thoughts of old.

If we do not challenge our beliefs and attitudes, as Socrates and others advise, we are abdicating to a past we likely had very little control over.

Worse, without realizing it, we are ordering up more of the same for the future. It's like riding in the back seat of life, deferring to an automatic pilot that, without periodic reprogramming, will tend to drive in circles, repeating the behaviors of yesterday in the lock-step march Freud labeled our "compulsion to repetition." Synaptic efficacy will see to it.

If you're happy with the way your life has been going, then relax and enjoy the ride. But if you're tiring of the same old outcomes and the same old conversations, it's time to vacate the back seat and regain control. That's what this book is all about;

helping you grab hold of the reins of your life and putting you back in the driver's seat, arming you with a prerecorded sixty-second commercial that you can use to regain control of your life's unforgiving minutes. As Kipling so insightfully observed, "If you can fill the unforgiving minute, yours is the earth and everything that's in it." By the time we're done here, and with a little practice, you'll be surprised how many minutes in the average day are capable of being influenced. And synaptic efficacy being what it is, the best way to ensure your success is to start early — the first minute every morning. The more you darken the lines of your new engrams, the more easily they will come to mind. In time, they will become the new automatic thoughts that will shape and trigger your feelings, perceptions and interpretations. Until that time, a conscious effort on your part will be required.

Let's begin.

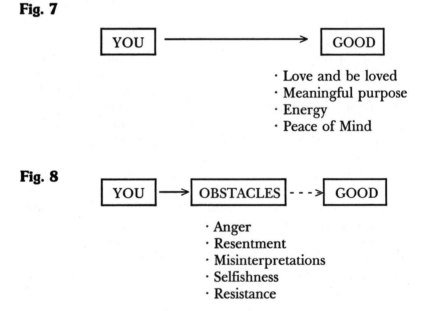

Fig. 7

YOU ──────────► GOOD

· Love and be loved
· Meaningful purpose
· Energy
· Peace of Mind

Fig. 8

YOU ─► OBSTACLES ‑ ‑ ‑► GOOD

· Anger
· Resentment
· Misinterpretations
· Selfishness
· Resistance

Fig. 9

· Positive attitudes & beliefs
· Positive self-esteem
· Positive self-direction

Fig. 10

Fig. 11

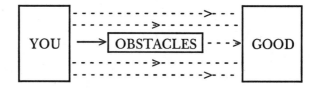

Notes:
[1]Paul Kurtz, *Exuberance - A Philosophy of Happiness*, (Buffalo: Prometheous Books, 1977), p. 172.
[2]M. Scott Peck, *The Road Less Traveled*, (New York: Simon & Schuster, 1978), p. 230.

Chapter 10

GETTING STARTED

The CHANGE graphic in Figure 12 depicts a few early milestones in life, focusing on events typically experienced by people age twenty to thirty-five. But change is an ongoing process, from conception to last breath. The key is how much of the change we drive ourselves or merely "accept." Someone once said we don't necessarily get what we want from life, only what we'll accept. Many of us are conditioned to be far too accepting. We seem to approach life with what Dr. Irene Kassorla describes in her book *Go For It* as a Five-Hundred Year Plan...living the first hundred years for your parents, the second hundred for your nice friends and neighbors, the third hundred for the children, the fourth for some cause you value and the fifth for you.[1] The problem is, you never get around to you.

If we accept the premise that the quality of our relationships largely determine the quality of our lives, and that we are only capable of recreating with another the nature of the relationship we have with ourselves, to have a good and rewarding life we have to learn to put ourselves first. This is not selfishness, it is preparation for life and for happiness.

Martin Buber, the late Jewish philosopher, had a marvelous point of view on change — what he described as the process of

"becoming." Buber contrasts the confining, restrictive "I-It" outlook — erroneously seeing yourself and others as finished products with set abilities and limits — with the unrestrained "I-Thou" viewpoint, where we nurture and affirm a vision of everything we and others plan on becoming. Buber saw life as a procession of "meetings," ideally where two people come together and confirm each others "Thou."

Referring to God as the "Eternal-Thou," Buber advised that "he who goes out with his whole being to meet his Thou...finds Him (the Eternal-Thou) who cannot be sought. It is a finding without a seeking." Buber taught that no prescription can lead us to that ultimate meeting with the "Eternal-Thou" and so none leads from it:

> ...a man does not pass from the moment of the
> supreme meeting the same being as he entered into
> it. Man receives not a specific content but a
> Presence, a Presence as power...with an inexpress-
> ible confirmation of meaning, one that desires
> confirmation in this life. This meaning can be
> received but not experienced...can be proved true
> by each man only in the singleness of his being and
> his life...We have "known" it, but we acquire no
> knowledge from it...we cannot explain it...we can
> only go and confirm its truth.[2]

Buber concluded that "full mutuality was not inherent in our life on earth...it is a grace for which one must always be ready and which one never gains as an assured possession."[3] He felt the secret was to go out with your full being to meet your Thou — to become the best that you can be and to encourage the same in others.

Our ability to grow and move forward in life becomes a function of focus. Resolving and learning from our past, we clear our mental circuitry to focus on the present; free to become creatively alive in the moment and free to "meet" others now that we have finally met ourselves. Far from being selfish, it is along this path of enlightened self-interest that personal freedom and personal fulfillment are to be found. It is the very path we are on now together.

IMPLEMENTATION

To help you get back out in front of your thoughts — back in the driver's seat — you're now in a position to begin applying what you've learned. It's time to turn the table on synaptic efficacy and get it working for you. What you'll be doing is seeding your thoughts with positive, goal-oriented statements. As you review these affirmations as part of a new daily regimen — as your sixty-second commercial gets aired — you'll actually be darkening the lines of a few new engrams. You'll discipline yourself to think these thoughts for the first few weeks, until the new thought pathways are etched and begin to recur on their own.

One word of caution. Do not expect immediate results. It takes time for the darkened-line engrams of old to fade and for your new affirmations and guided visualizations to gain a beachhead in your mind. Dr. Maltz was very specific about the time investment required to change your thoughts and your self-image. "It usually requires a minimum of 21 days to effect any perceptible change in a mental image. Following plastic surgery it takes about 21 days for the average patient to get used to his new face. When an arm or leg is amputated the 'phantom limb' persists for about 21 days."[4]

Maltz goes on to suggest that the same phenomenon is behind why it takes about three weeks for a new house to begin to "seem like home." The message is clear. Give yourself a full three weeks for the new thoughts and imagery to jell in your mind. In the interim, try not to second-guess the process. Do your best to suspend judgment and try not to monitor your progress too closely. Just let it happen.

The power of hypnosis is the power of belief. The subject behaves differently because he thinks and believes differently. The mental handcuffs that limit us have the same power over us as the hypnotist's words do over a hypnotized subject. Just as we acquired our current beliefs without effort, so too will we acquire the new replacement beliefs in a relaxed condition. Effort in this realm is counterproductive. This is not a muscling exercise, but an etching process where the grooves respond to repetition, not to pressure.

Conscious thought is the control knob or conduit into your subconscious mind. That's how inappropriate beliefs gained access and how your replacement thoughts and beliefs will get similarly anchored. Just remember, it's going to take three weeks to set the anchor.

DROPPING THE LOG

There's an old saying in the business community that "nothing happens until somebody sells someone or something." The adage applies here as well. Back in Chapter 2 we discussed the importance of commitment and focus, that by committing to a goal you feel passionately about, you begin to access an ancient wiring system — a wiring system that will not only keep you pointed and on course but will put you in touch with the energy and the conviction you'll need to stay the course. You get there by selling yourself on the direction, the "iasm" passkey we reviewed in Chapter 3.

The jumping-off point is a milestone event. If it were to be depicted in Figure 12, a rendering of a light bulb would seem appropriate. It is the point when you finally realize and acknowledge what it is you want to do. Exactly where the bulb gets inserted in your milestone map will vary with the individual. Wherever it falls, embrace it and honor it.

We characterized the act of publicly committing to a goal as being comparable to dropping a log at a river's bend. The human brain and central nervous system together are a success-seeking, goal-driven mechanism that require a goal to function properly. And to set the goal in your mind, it helps to repeatedly picture yourself in the process of attaining it, thereby recruiting your subconscious into the campaign as well.

Since confidence and self-image are derived from real-life action — from "experiencing" — our strategy is to simulate that action through repetitive visualizations. Much like the principle of the Syber Vision program, your ability to mimic the behavior so pictured grows in time as your ancient wiring system converts the information from visual to behavioral prompts. All the while you are strengthening your belief and conviction that this is right for you...that this is home.

Martin Buber had a marvelous outlook on life. He believed that God is in continual contact with each and everyone of us; that God speaks to us through daily events. In Buber's words, "Happening upon happening, situation upon situation, are enabled and empowered by the personal speech of God to demand of the human person that he take his stand and make his decision."[5]

It may well be time to take your stand. No one can know for sure but you. No one is wired to your applause meter but you. Your continued presence here would suggest it is in fact time and you are ready. As David Viscott cautioned earlier, "The final push is a 'lonely act,' for no one can know or understand what you are 'becoming' but yourself."[6] As you prepare to make that proverbial "leap," take comfort in knowing that you have the best of allies behind you, someone who knows you better than anyone else on earth and who you know and trust will be there at crunch time...yes, YOURSELF.

Once you've sold yourself, have gained possession of the "iasm" passkey, and have dropped your log — made your commitment — the "should do" voices in your life will fade as they and the world adjust to your new reality; a reality that starts as a dream and, like the log at the river's bend, eventually traps and diverts enough resources to profoundly alter the typography of your life.

PRACTICE

As any coach or trainer will tell you, it's important to practice as you intend to play. If you expect to play with intensity, you must practice with intensity, and if you intend to sell your opponent on your capabilities on game day, you have to start by selling yourself at practice. It doesn't work any other way. The Dolphins of 1972 were living proof.

You can't expect your mind and body to execute on command until you've committed the activity to memory through endless repetition. Otherwise the conscious mind will interfere and impede your performance. You'll know in your heart you're not fully prepared and doubt will pre-empt conviction, clogging your mind and impeding your performance.

Various professional athletes over time have described a level of performance that has an almost mystical quality; where they have a sense of "knowing" just before it happens, where time seems to slow down and where their performance seems effortless and flawless. They call it performing "in the zone." Investigations into the phenomenon have tended to find the common denominator to be a conscious mind that has been quieted. Athletes who have so trained their bodies and minds, when called upon to perform, are able to quiet the chatter in their minds, freeing themselves from any mental or emotional distraction.

New research into the brain has monitored an interesting relationship between skill level and brain activity. Surprisingly, as the subject's skill level increased the metabolic rate of the brain slowed down. Consistent with this have been findings that higher levels of brain metabolism correlate with worse performance. The one exception to this has been in the visual cortex — the part of the brain that processes visual imagery. Here the metabolic rate increases with skill development, suggesting that the subject is able to process more visual information as his or her skill increases.

Once you debut your one-minute commercial and amass at least twenty-one days of repetition and refinement, you'll find your thoughts, feelings and actions begin to converge. Gradually, you'll be in a better position to quiet your conscious mind and gain access to that ancient wiring system; the same wiring system that will enhance your ability to listen and taken on input, often slowing time in the process and releasing a form of euphoric energy — energy born from accomplishment and from the growing realization and conviction that you can recreate your life.

You do not need to be a professional athlete to avail yourself of these benefits. Once sampled, you will gladly embrace a regimen that promises continued access to the zone, to the balanced calmness that is endemic there, and to the energy and mood-enhancing feelings triggered when you find yourself making headway on an important goal. This is a frequent occurrence when in the zone.

You could build a case that the Dolphins' season in 1972 took place within the zone. Certainly there were selected games and key moments that qualified. To single out any one incident would tend to diminish the many fine performances — individual and team — that made up that unprecedented year. Yet one incident does come to mind and I offer it as an example of the whole.

It was early in the second period of the AFC Championship game against the Pittsburgh Steelers at Pittsburgh. As the Dolphin 1972 Yearbook would later attribute to Steeler John Fuqua, "when you come here you're playing 40 football players and 52,000 fans." [7] The Steelers scored first after intercepting an Earl Morrall pass. Unable to put a drive together in the first quarter, the Dolphins opened the second quarter by being blunted again. The combination of Franco Harris and his Italian Army, Gerela's Gorillas (Roy Gerela) and John Fuqua and his arm-band Legion was making its presence known. The Steel Curtain that was to stymie opponents later in the 1970s was already taking shape.

It was fourth-and-five and the Dolphins were in punt formation. Earl Morrall had done a remarkable job filling in for the injured Bob Griese for the previous ten games, but the Dolphin offense was flat. It needed a boost. The boost came in an unexpected fashion; unexpected, that is, if you weren't familiar with the Dolphins depth chart. With fourth-and-five at the Pittsburgh 49, Larry Seiple, number 20, was back to punt. Except on this play, number 20 did the unexpected. He took off and ran instead. No one on the field knew he was going to run. It was not a called play. He did it all on his own.

An excellent punter, Seiple had a runner's instincts. In fact, he was listed third on the depth chart at both the wide receiver and half-back positions. The man could run. He also was alert, prepared and ready. When the moment arose, he instinctively knew what to do. As Seiple explained after the game, "The keys are the men in the middle who usually wait. The Steelers didn't wait. They were turning to go back downfield to help with the return. So I took off. Heck, my own team didn't even know I was running."

Seiple needed to make 5 yards. If he didn't, he'd have to

run all the way to the airport rather than face Shula. Seiple made the 5 yards and 32 additional insurance yards as well as he raced to the Steelers 12-yard line. It was easier than running to the airport — a magical moment within a magical season. It happened because of Larry Seiple's level of preparedness and self-confidence. He was able to quiet his conscious mind so his visual cortex could let in the needed visual stimuli. Seiple was in the zone. When the opportunity arose, and the conditions were right, Larry Seiple was ready. And the Dolphins moved on to Super Bowl VII and their date with destiny.

The Dolphins' 1972 Yearbook and owner Joe Robbie described the time poetically:

> We have promises to keep. And miles to go before
> we sleep.   — Joseph Robbie

> It was the Miami dressing room, only minutes after
> the Dolphins had lost to Dallas in Super Bowl VI,
> that Joe Robbie, the Club's managing general
> partner reached into his despair for words written
> by the poet, Robert Frost.

> The entire year of 1972 - off season and regular
> season - would be devoted by Robbie, Coach Don
> Shula and the entire organization to fulfilling the
> promises and covering the miles. The target was
> sharply defined: Bring Miami a world champion-
> ship and the Vince Lombardi Trophy that goes to
> the Super Bowl victor.

> The challenge was there for everyone. Robbie,
> Shula, the players. Some players, such as
> cornerback Tim Foley, relied on a more visual
> approach as a reminder, hanging a photograph of
> the scoreboard for Super Bowl VI in his home.

> "The clock reads zero seconds and the score reads
> Dallas 24, Miami 3" Foley explained when he
> returned to training camp. "At least once a day
> since the Super Bowl I've taken a long, long look at
> that picture to help me remember what I felt like

after that game, and how I don't want to feel that way again."

And so with poems and pictures reminding them of their dark hour in New Orleans the year before, the Dolphins prepared for Super Bowl VII against the Washington Redskins, knowing that their 16-0 record meant little if it wasn't embellished by a triumph at Los Angeles.

"We had all our eggs in one basket," acknowledged Shula. "If we had lost, everything we had worked for would have been destroyed. Sixteen and one - you have critics. Seventeen and zero - there's no doubt."

On January 14, 1972 in Super Bowl VII, the Dolphins left no doubt, fulfilling the promises and covering the miles remaining with a convincing 14-7 victory over the Redskins that annexed the world championship and the first undefeated season in the history of the National Football League.

"It is," said Robbie afterward, "the greatest single achievement in the history of sports."[8]

Joe Robbie likely never heard about Pavlov's passion and gradualness injunctive. He didn't have to. He knew it intuitively, particularly the gradualness piece. It took seven years, four months and twenty-six days from the time the franchise was granted for Robbie and his organization to make it to the top. Record time, but still seven-plus years. Robbie worked hard, assembled the necessary resources and he persevered.

The Dolphins' achievement in 1972 is there for all to learn from. If there was a map of the process, it would read:

Change what you THINK ABOUT, TALK ABOUT, VISU-ALIZE and DO

Change what you BELIEVE and EXPECT

CHANGE what you BECOME.

Buried deep within each of us is a giant river with a strong and definite current. Where do you find it? If you look closely, there have been clues in your life all along the way. Review your past achievements and the things that make your heart sing. You can only operate in the zone if you're on the right playing field for you. How do you get there? You get there by identifying your motivational pattern and committing to a direction that leverages that pattern and facilitates your becoming the person you were created to be. Your new direction respects your inborn preferences and rhythms and brings the rest of your life into conformity. Between your index cards and your sixty-second commercial, you're a natural to succeed. The pieces are all in place.

Your daily efforts at practicing and visualizing the contents of your cards will begin to etch the necessary new pathways in your mind and consciousness. In time, your thoughts will naturally gravitate there and you'll begin to embody and become the person you were meant to be.

REHEARSAL

If you haven't already done so, go back and transcribe your goal work sheets over to the recommended index cards. Now is the time to tighten down on your goals. Sort out those that would be nice and focus in on those that are essential to you. An old axiom from the business world suggests that "more than two objectives are no objectives." With that refinement in mind, go back through the five boxes in Chapter 7 and transfer the surviving statements over to five actual index cards. You'll be spending a bit of time with them so make them neat and pleasing to the eye.

The final two cards — I AM IN THE PROCESS OF BECOMING...and THEREFORE, REMEMBER TO... — comprise the narrative script pool for your commercial. Take them in hand now and read them over. Find a quiet room where you can block out the world and reflect on the qualities or attributes you've listed as well as the activities you believe will lead you there. Spot check your applause meter to ensure it is responding favorably to the "intended direction," and that the thought of committing to this goal stirs your passions and begins to swell your expectations.

As your thoughts begin to swirl, press fast forward and picture yourself at the precise moment when your new goal is attained. Scan the scene in your mind's eye taking note of all evident detail. Hear and see the background noise and the people in attendance. Zoom in on yourself and feel yourself responding to the achievement. Stay with the visual until you see and begin to physically experience a release and surge of feelings. These same winning feelings will captivate and energize you at the real occasion.

Pause to honor and embrace these marvelous, uplifting feelings. Pull as much of it back to the present as possible. As you do, the visual will of necessity begin to fade. As it does, focus on the audio portion which intrusively begins to proclaim the content of the two index cards in your hand. You can use either your own voice or your favorite broadcast announcer. The key is to express your goals as present-tense facts, not hoped-for possibilities someday down the road.

As the voice trails off, repeat the earlier visual as best you can. If accolades are involved, stay with the reprised visual until you hear, see and feel the applause. See yourself acknowledging and responding to whatever form the recognition takes. Last but not least, zero in on how good you're feeling about yourself. Grab hold of the feeling and pull it with you back to the present. Allow its energy to invigorate and spur you on.

Put the book down and try it now. Until you commit the words to memory, feel free to read the cards. Gradually the words and visuals will integrate and appear as if on cue. If you doubt you can do it, just relax and give it a try. You've probably done the same thing in the negative arena dozens of times. Who among us hasn't allowed a picture of some feared, dreaded event to enter our mind causing our hands to sweat and our stomachs to get queasy. What you'll be doing here is crossing over to the positive side of the street and letting your imagination take it from there. It's nothing more than a guided daydream with a beginning, a middle and an end, and a happy end at that.

Repeat the sequence a few times until you get the hang of it. It's really quite simple and the effect on your psyche can and will be profound. You'll be particularly impressed by the commercials portability. You can invoke your new friend anytime and anywhere...and you will.

BEGINNING

Once you've rehearsed your commercial, you'll begin to see how inherently natural the program is. It's nothing more than an organized daydream with a prewritten script and a viable story line. The only thing that remains is your commitment and resolve to stick with it for at least three weeks. My advice is simple and compact. Commit to do it, not try it, and don't begin until you're ready to muster a full-court press. If you can begin with that level of resolve, you'll be setting out on the most exciting chapter of your life — one destined to stir your passions and renew your spirit, bringing you back in touch with feelings and rumblings that you may have long since forgotten.

Remember, you're working on deepening and rekindling your "power of belief." Like the 1972 Miami Dolphins, you're looking to cross that magical threshold where your belief transforms into conviction, your grip on the "iasm" passkey becomes vise-like, and your dreams turn into expectations and your expectations shape and empower your reality.

The key is to begin each day with your sixty-second commercial, remembering that the action and the results you seek begin in your mind. As John Keats intuitively observed, "Well begun is half done." In time we all come to realize that the present — the here and now — is all we ever really have. To help you keep conscious hold of that fact, the program emphasizes the importance of priming your pump on a daily basis by acknowledging and managing the most important minute of your new life — the first minute every morning. Why the first minute? Because of its "freshness" and the clean-slate feeling that accompanies the dawn of each new day; because of its ability to profoundly influence the balance of that day, enabling us to begin the progression of events we call "the day" on a positive track and with a sense of direction, mission and purpose.

Part of this thing we call the human condition is our tendency to go with the flow, typically a flow initiated by others. To repeatedly talk about something, anticipate it, and perhaps even curse it, in the process, we perpetuate it. This continues at least until we become more alert to where we let our prevalent thoughts and conversations go and until we regain control by replacing those limiting, confining thoughts of yesterday with the words and visuals from our sixty-second commercial — thoughts and pictures of our best self in the process of excelling and striving. We can then be awakened to the invigorating possibilities within reach now that we've released ourselves from prison...a prison we may not have erected but that our thoughts helped perpetuate and empower.

Robert Bly, the poet, has some marvelous descriptions of this process of rejuvenation whereby we take hold of our life and "awaken our King." Bly likens the process to getting the doorknobs of your life on your side of the door. He faults the naive men and women who fail to choose, allowing the events of life to choose for them. In his book *Iron John*, Bly quotes these telling lines from Richard Wilbur's poem about Don Quixote's random ride where, as he approached a crossroad, Quixote wished his horse would choose for him:

> "...For glory lay wherever he might turn
> His head was light with pride
> His horse's shoes were heavy
> and he headed for the barn."[9]

From Bly's perspective, our job is to not only free ourselves from family cages and collective mind sets but to release transcendent beings from imprisonment and trance.

THE UNFORGIVING MINUTE

Up to this point, your attention has been centered on remembering to invoke your sixty-second commercial the first minute each day. While this continues to be the central focus, and rightfully so, I'd like to shift the discussion to what Rudyard Kipling described as the "unforgiving minute."

In his classic poem *If*, in which he imparts fatherly advice to his son on becoming a man, Kipling describes over a dozen situations calling for restraint, trust, patience, forgiveness, resilience, loss, renewal, heart, determination, independence, perspective and balance. He concludes his litany of virtuosity with the following lines:

> "...If you can fill the unforgiving minute
>   With sixty seconds worth of distance run,
>   Yours is the Earth and everything that's in it..."

Kipling's meaning and core advice are revealed in the opening line of the poem "If you can keep your head when all about you are losing theirs." Despite what the world throws your way, keep your thoughts under control, your temperament balanced and your eye on your goal. That way, when confronted by one of life's unexpected but inevitable distractions or unpleasantries, you'll be able to confront the unforgiving minute and use the time well, squeezing and milking it for the full sixty seconds.

Your new sixty-second commercial is a versatile tool that will help you heed Kipling's advice whenever and wherever an unforgiving minute arises. As Kipling himself intuitively understood, **THE ACTION BEGINS IN YOUR MIND.**

> "If you can keep your head when all about you
>   Are losing theirs...
>   If you can fill the unforgiving minute...
>   Yours is the Earth and everything that's in it..."

NOTES:
[1] Dr. Irene Kassorla, *Go For It*, (New York: Delacorte Press, 1984), p. 3.
[2] Martin Buber, *I and Thou*, (New York: Charles Scribner's Sons, 1958), pp. 110-111.
[3] Ibid. p. 131.
[4] Dr. Maxwell Maltz, *Psycho-Cybernetics*, (New York: Simon & Schuster, 1960), p. xiii.
[5] Buber, pp. 136-137.
[6] Dr. David Viscott, *Risking*, (New York: Simon & Schuster, 1977), p. 207.
[7] Miami Dolphins, Ltd., 1972 Dolphins Yearbook, p. 141.
[8] Ibid. p. 147.
[9] Robert Bly, *Iron John*, (New York: Addison-Wesley, 1990), p. 176.

EPILOGUE

Towards the end of Chapter 5 I slipped in a quote from John Townsend Trowbridge that deserved considerably more comment than I gave it at the time. Let's pause to honor it now.

"Not in rewards, but in the strength to strive,
   the blessing lies."

There's a wealth of advice and wisdom buried in these dozen words. There's a message about materialism, fortitude, purpose, spirituality and mortality. And beneath it all, a strong pre-emptive message emerges centering on just one word — ENERGY.

According to Trowbridge, the real pleasure in life is being able to strive, and that suggests energy and vigor — energy and vigor to sustain the effort and to tolerate the setbacks; energy and vigor to keep moving forward when the world suggests we roll over and quit; and energy and vigor to follow our heart's desires when the "should do" voices unite and point elsewhere.

Where will we access such an inexhaustible supply of energy? The answer is in two places. First, the energy is found in a sizeable and strong eddy that accompanies the main current in your life, a whirlpool of energy that only your applause meter and your "iasm" passkey can locate and penetrate. The balance of the energy you'll draw from your commitment and investment in your one-minute pep talk.

Imagery is a technique to generate new experience and the energy that typically accompanies it. Instead of simply reacting to future experiences, you'll be helping to create and empower them, first in your mind then in the day to day flow of your life.

Our map then is complete:

Change what you THINK ABOUT, TALK ABOUT, VISUALIZE & DO

Change what you BELIEVE & EXPECT

Change what you BECOME

On the input side of the equation, we defined the acronym P.E.P. to underscore what was required from you:

Preparation
Enthusiasm
Permission

On the output side, as we arrive at the finish line, we can redefine the term to describe the rewards the program is designed to prompt and elicit. Namely:

Perspective and purpose
Energy
Peace of mind

THE ACTION BEGINS IN YOUR MIND. As you progress through the initial twenty-one days of your program, striving to etch in your thoughts and behavior what you have captured on your cards and in your one-minute pep talk, you will begin to observe and experience the concept of progressive realization. You will be opening more and more space in your life for the envisioned achievements and events to gradually take place as you anchor a new, casual chain. This chain will influence your expectations, and in time will lead to a wondrous growth in your power of belief, your will to prepare and in your propulsion to begin and to persevere — all component and defining attributes of the "strength to strive."

The next move is yours. Remember, **THE ACTION BE-GINS IN YOUR MIND.**

> "When you are advancing confidently in the direction of your own dreams, and you're endeavoring to live the life which you have imagined, then you will meet with a success unexpected in common hours."
>
> — Henry David Thoreau

Good luck, God speed and pass it on.

APPENDIX

MY BELIEFS

I believe..............in me
...in what I am in the process of becoming
...that God is in my corner
...in the power of a smile and a hug
...in living with passion and commitment
...in love and compassion
...in second chances
...in looking for the GOOD
...in self-actualization
...in The M.E. Weekend & The One-Minute P.E.P. Talk
...that the action begins in my mind
...in managing the unforgiving minutes of my life

MY GOALS

Overall....　to gather the collective wisdom of past and present thinkers for the purpose of enriching lives.

Family.....　to build self-esteem daily in my three sons.

Career.....　to invest myself daily in The One-Minute P.E.P. Talk and M.E. Weekend activities.

Mental.....　to reaffirm my own self-esteem through daily practice of my goal cards and my one-minute pep talk.

Physical...　to avoid food and drink that impair my thoughts and moods, and to maintain three times/week exercise program.

Social.....　to practice "meeting" daily.

Community..to help others encountering difficulties along the way.

Spiritual..　to integrate God in all of the above.

MY "BE-ATTITUDES"

To work and practice each day to be...

...a proponent and model of self-actualization
...faithful to me and to my needle readings
...a good friend and father to my boys
...creatively alive in the moment
...a good listener...and to "meet"
...dedicated to the truth...to undoing the tyranny
   of pre-conception
...a help to others

I AM IN THE PROCESS OF BECOMING...

...a published author
...an effective public speaker
...a self-actualization advocate
...a catalyst for "meeting"
...a thoughtful father
...a good friend
...synonymous with The M.E. Weekend and
   The One-Minute P.E.P. Talk

THEREFORE, REMEMBER TO...

...Listen <u>In</u>
...Act on my needle readings
...Get my heart into it and <u>commit</u>
...Practice my one-minute pep talk daily
...Look for the GOOD in others and in the
   moment
...Emphasize loving, not being loved
...Remember that the action begins in my
   mind

PART II

THE ME ENCOUNTER

*A Journey of
Self-Discovery and Self-Renewal*

PROLOGUE

"Of all sad words of tongue or pen
the saddest are these
...(what) might have been."

— John Greenleaf Whittier

These haunting words strike deep, particularly for the person not fully in touch with him or herself, the person who should be happy, but often is not, and the person still struggling to find peace with him or herself.

In the process of growing up amidst the pressures to conform and gain parental acceptance and approval, many of us lose touch with ourselves. For whatever reason, our true feelings are sublimated and we go into hiding or into a prolonged sleepwalk. The damage is a loss of intimacy — first with ourselves, then with others.

While the attainment of material possessions receives plenty of play in the media, it's the quality of our relationships that largely determines the quality of our lives. Since we are only capable of re-creating with another the nature of the relationship we have with ourselves, we first need to understand, accept and love ourselves before we can truly and fully love another; before the attainment of those coveted possessions can begin to deliver the hoped-for happiness and peace of mind.

Our uniquely American culture, with its emphasis on individual effort, personal accomplishment and spirited competition, has prompted enormous advances in medicine, industrial technology and space exploration. It has also spawned a growing

121

number of people who can't keep up, who don't even try or who get lost along the way; people who never find their niche or who temporarily get derailed in the process; people who are not at peace with themselves and whose relationships suffer for it.

This hidden cost of America's pursuit of excellence in no way invalidates the great American experiment. It only suggests it's time that more of our energy and attention be marshalled and directed to spotlighting and solving the problem.

The Me Encounter is a direct frontal assault against this spiritual erosion and drift; against what many consider to be the most widespread disease in America today — namely, self-doubt and a growing identity vacuum.

Employing a technique known as a "guided fantasy walk," you are about to embark on an insight-laden experience. I urge you to suspend your disbelief and to embrace the opportunity about to unfold. Open yourself to reconnect with a person — a very special person — who may well hold the key to unlocking your future happiness, someone who will function as your Guide in the pages ahead.

The Me Encounter and *The Strength to Strive*, together, are intended to provide a restorative and energizing experience by bringing back much of the freedom of choice and the freedom to change that may have been lost in early childhood; getting you back in touch with the sense of wonder, adventure and self-worth that might have been left behind as well. You will be free to become creatively alive in the moment and free to meet others now that you have finally met yourself.

Please pick up a pencil and permit yourself to go with the imagery and mood about to be created. Your rewards will be bountiful. Just as in life, you'll get back from this experience in direct proportion to what you put in.

Let the magic flow back into your life. Do it for you. You deserve it. Do it now. It's time.

INTRODUCTION

One of the hallmarks of Ed Koch's mayoralty in New York City during the 1980s was his habit of asking "How am I doing so far?" A fair question. In time, a question we all likely will ask of ourselves or, worse, have thrust upon us by one of life's unforeseen but inevitable twists or jolts. Whichever brought you here today, I bid you a warm welcome.

Perhaps it has been a long time since you passed this way, or perhaps, like painting the back of the garage, you always intended to find the time but never did. Either way, congratulations and relax...you're about to get it done.

I believe there is a natural tendency to teach ourselves what we most need to learn and remember. What you are about to read and experience was pivotal in launching my own renewal — or second wind if you will — and is likewise aimed at helping you get back in touch with your deep, innermost feelings, recovering yourself as a whole person in the process.

This book is not intended to replace counseling. Some may find it a useful tool to use within their counseling sessions; others will benefit from it as a freestanding experience. Whatever your need and intended usage, as in life, you will get out what you put in. You're about to meet yourself as ABC Sports would say "up close and personal." I'm betting, on balance, you'll like what you see.

As we set out on this journey together, I'm reminded of the after-dinner speaker who had prepared a thirty-minute talk. On the way to the podium, he's told the program is running late, so could he please limit himself to ten minutes. Unfazed, he pockets his script and utters, "Well let's see, we've only got ten minutes, where should I start?" Before he can frame his own response, a comedian in the back shouts out, "Start at the ninth minute!"

While we are not similarly time-constrained here, I do appreciate the time pressures we're all under and the resulting tendency to look for shortcuts; like perhaps starting at the ninth minute by reading the wrap-up chapters first. To do so here would be to rob yourself of a rich, experiential opportunity. I liken it to the difference between driving through a neighborhood and walking through. One is removed, aloof and sealed off, while the other is open to all the sights, sounds, smells and subtle textures.

What do you say we call a personal time-out, park our respective cars and go for a walk together? The Neighborhood we'll be walking through is in sight. If it looks familiar, it should. The Neighborhood is YOU.

Yes, our careers, families, religious beliefs and hometowns are subjects of the utmost importance to us. Environmental protection, disarmament, abortion and AIDS are all subjects that may strike deep and stir our emotions. Yet, none carry the importance and wield the immense power to influence how we relate to our respective worlds than one subject in particular. This subject very rarely gets diagnosed and talked about yet transcends all others; namely, how YOU think as an individual and how YOU have been conditioned to see the world.

What we will be doing in the chapters ahead is to give this most important of all subjects the air time, emphasis and attention it intrinsically warrants. As Theologian Alan Jones described in his book *Journey Into Christ*, "When it comes to important questions of meaning and purpose, I cannot accept second-hand information...that learned from a parent, friend, doctor or spouse. There has to be a personal word, a unique confrontation, if I am to come alive."[1] The M.E. Weekend is just such a unique confrontation.

There are but two pre-requisites for your journey to be productive: a strong desire to get back in touch with yourself is the first and the ability to think deep, clear thoughts is the second.

Let's take them one at a time.

#1. A strong desire to get back in touch with yourself:

In the process of becoming an adult, many of us grow up feeling "different" and aren't sure why or what to do about it. For any number of reasons we may have lost touch with our true, inner selves. As Robert Bly might observe, the doorknob doesn't seem to be on our side of the door. Getting back in touch with ourselves — relocating that doorknob — is achievable if we're willing to do our part and put forth the effort...in our case today, willing to pick up a pencil.

The biblical story of Lazarus being raised from the dead, described in the 11th Chapter of John, addresses this very point. Guarding and blocking the entrance to Lazarus' tomb was a large stone. Jesus was deeply moved by the pain of Mary and Martha, Lazarus' sisters, and asked those assembled to "Take away the stone." Moving the stone himself would have been a minor event compared to raising Lazarus from the dead, but Jesus insisted those present put forth some effort too.

We all likely have stones holding back miracles in our own lives; stones of self-doubt, unforgiveness or disbelief. As you approach the opportunity about to unfold here, view it as an opportunity to regain control of your life and to put forth an effort — a uniquely personal effort — to "take away the stone" that may be blocking your forward progress, preventing you from becoming the person you were meant to be.

#2. The ability to think deep, clear thoughts:

This may seem like an obvious motherhood, but don't be too quick to assume you fully qualify. Clarity of thought, vigor and spiritual insights and awakenings aren't possible until the body is balanced and free of stress...the stress we trigger by our thoughts and interpretations and the stress we cause by what we eat and drink.

One of the lyrics from Billy Joel's song "A Matter of Trust" states "You can't go the distance with too much resistance." Other than the French during World War II and Thomas Edison in his quest for light, resistance has not been a friend to man. The next few paragraphs are intended to make you uncomfortable; to give you pause to think and to consider if one or more of the sources of resistance described here could be causing you trouble.

The body you inhabit is a miraculous and wondrous structure, composed of complex organs and intricate support systems, all ingeniously intertwined and regulated by a delicate balance of chemicals. One life substance that seems to be central, that acts as an on-board gyroscope for the rest of the body, is our blood-sugar level. Our bodies are essentially machines. They are activated by energy and require periodic refueling. Our stomach and digestive tracks process this fuel — the food and drink we ingest — extracting the nutrients that can power the body and expelling the balance. The human body is a highly efficient power plant.

When wholesome foods, particularly carbohydrates, are eaten, they are slowly broken down into glucose (sugar) and the excess is stored in the liver as glycogen. The efficient functioning of the brain, one of the biggest users of sugar in the body, is dependent on a stable and level sugar supply in the bloodstream. A problem can arise when refined sugars or carbohydrates are consumed. Since these "refined" products have been broken down or processed from multiple sugar chains (polysaccharides) to single sugar molecules (monosaccharides), once eaten they are quickly absorbed into the bloodstream without need for further digestion. The result is a rapid and significant rise in blood sugar. Because of the pivotal role blood sugar plays, other bodily systems are activated to bring the sugar level back into balance. All the while, messages from the brain controlling mood, motivation, appetite and learning are vulnerable to being disrupted and corrupted. The result can be a burst of temper, aggression, and anti-social behavior, as well as depression, mood swings, distorted thinking, food cravings, fatigue and irritability.

While sugar is perhaps the worst disrupter of this delicate body chemistry, substances such as caffeine, nicotine, alcohol and selected allergens can trigger similar unbalancing. Rather than greeting each new day with a zestful bounce, eager for the challenges ahead, many of us are recovering from yesterday's chemical roller coaster ride. Our bodies get consumed in an unnecessary civil war. For those affected, they awaken to find their bodies adding to their list of problems rather than being their most staunch ally.

What sort of problems you ask? The afflictions are many, much the same as those brought on by stress; not surprising when you realize that the effect of eating the wrong foods is to place the body under tremendous stress. Symptoms can range from recurring headaches, backaches, allergies, joint pains, low energy, difficulty concentrating, bouts of anxiety, irritability and general malaise.

If you are experiencing even a little quiver of doubt this might apply to you, I urge you to check it out. Denial is a formidable opponent and its best friend is procrastination. Together they can immobilize you. Take a moment now — right now — and go through the addictive substances one by one:

✓ Sugar	✓ Nicotine
✓ Sweetened Foods	✓ Tranquilizers/Sleeping Pills
✓ Caffeine	✓ Marijuana/Cocaine/Uppers
✓ Alcohol	✓ Opiate narcotics

Be as honest with yourself as you can be. Might you have a problem? Ask your parents, spouse or friends to help muster as much candor as possible.

Why am I taking the time for this? Because I want you to be able to think deep, clear thoughts; to be able to process information and retain it; to be open to all the wonders that life has to offer and to the insights that hopefully await you in the pages ahead; and to be free of the muffling, distorted haze of addiction and any impairment to your senses, thoughts and perceptions. Ideally, I'd like to see you there before you begin the M.E. Weekend exercises. With but one life to live, don't waste it being pulled down by a needless civil war that can cloud your thinking, block your happiness and blunt your growth. Let the sunshine back into your life. A bookmark will hold your place until you're ready to return. The balance of your journey will be that much more productive.

> "Let us go then, you and I
>   when the evening is set out against the sky
>   like a patient etherized upon the table."
>   — T. S. Elliott - *The Love Song To J. Alfred Pruefrock*

These opening lines of T. S. Elliott's caught my fancy over twenty-five years ago. Only now do I understand why. They were a precursor of a journey I would take that would forever alter my life. The journey you and I are setting out upon — right now — together.

NOTE:
[1] Alan Jones, *Journey Into Christ*, (New York: Seabury Press, 1977), pp. 91-92.

Section 1

THE M.E.
(Me Encounter)
WEEKEND

Chapter 1

THE REUNION

"Let us go then, you and I
when the evening is set out against the sky
like a patient etherized upon the table."
— T.S. Elliott - *The Love Song to J. Alfred Pruefrock*

A mist has settled in around the perimeter of the Neighbor-hood. You enter without hesitation leaving your escort behind. Your eyes are fixed upon the solitary figure who has emerged to be your guide. His or her features are not yet vis-ible through the fog, but the stature is small. Perhaps it is a child.

As you strain to make out features, you feel a strange sense of release. It's as if the mist were cleansing you of current pres-sures and worries.

On occasion in the past, you've sensed the presence of a Higher Power in your life. Those occasions were generally marked by a strong after-the-fact awareness; a sort of hindsight clarity that you had in fact just been blessed and empowered by a spiritual experience.

Today is different. With each step forward you instinctively sense something special is about to happen. You feel strangely peaceful and eager to proceed. It's as if someone called a "time-out" in your life and you've been given a few days for rest and reflection. You sense the grace and blessings to come. You're struck by an intense feeling of inner peace, embracing it like you would an old friend who surprises you with a visit.

Your Guide is within speaking distance now and the facial features have become clear. It is a child. A very special child.

You are both rendered speechless as you gaze upon each other. Words are not necessary and would only interfere with this unexpected reunion. For a split second you feel riveted to the ground, then instinctively vault forward with open arms. The child's eyes speak volumes to you. The child is you at age eight.

You hold the hug for a few precious seconds, unclear how such a meeting is possible, but joyous for this opportunity to remember and to reconnect. As if on cue, you both step back and are spellbound by the sight of the other. Your heart has sung before, but never quite like this. An immense wide-eyed smile is threatening to crease your face permanently. What a marvelous moment.

As you turn and head toward town hand in hand, you become aware that a number of similar reunions have happened simultaneously all across town. Men and women and their youthful counterparts are all converging on the town green. A large banner has been stretched over the entry way. It reads "Welcome to the M.E. Weekend." The atmosphere is alive with expectation and nostalgia.

As you take your seats on the makeshift benches, you are handed a notebook and pencil — one set for the two of you. What is striking about the gathering is that each twosome seems oblivious to the presence of the others except for a Moderator, who has just ascended the podium to call the group to order.

The Moderator is a kindly, older man who seems to embody the love and the caring that will characterize this two-day treasure trove. He surveys the audience and seems pleased to see the extent of the hand-holding and the snuggling already underway. He pauses to enjoy the sight, much like a proud grand-father who has passed this way before.

Moved by the group's evident joy, he clasps his hands and shakes them over his head, signaling both unity and triumph. The crowd grows quiet. "Ladies and gentlemen, to quote my friend John Keats 'Well begun is half done' and you dear people have certainly begun well."

His voice and manner are soothing, like a warm fire on a frigid night. "I congratulate each of you for the courage and conviction that have brought you this far. Rest assured your perseverance and effort will be returned to you multi-fold."

By now you're hanging on his every word. He continues the orientation. "Spend not your time questioning how this could be, but spend it in quiet reflection. Accept that your Higher Power has guided you here, to help you listen in to your inner thoughts, to get you back in touch with your true self. During your visit here you will have access to all the important people in your life, and the places and milestone events of your youth. You've met the special guide and companion who will accompany you on your journey — a journey of self-discovery and remembrance. The cleansing mist you experienced upon arrival has ensured that everything you say and hear will be from the heart without distortion. Your time here will pass quickly, so please use it well. Open yourself to all the wonders that await and your rewards will be many. Much of what you'll learn will flow from your own pencil now that you've decided to 'take away the stone.' "

You look down and notice there is someone who can't keep from staring at you. "Before we go any further, there is a young person at your side who is dying to ask you a few questions. Let's take a moment, get reacquainted, and address those pressing questions."

You turn and face your young Guide. You feel a new-found sense of completeness, as if a void in your inner core has finally been plugged. As you look into the eyes of this mirror of yesterday, you begin to remember the joys and the pains of your youth.

Chapter 2 ─────────

REMEMBRANCES

Editor's Note: You will need a pencil to complete portions of
this and subsequent chapters. To gain maximum
benefit, you may wish to set aside a quiet
weekend to devote to the reflective exercises,
opening yourself to the many insights that await.
If you've borrowed the book from a friend or
the library, you'll want to record your answers
in a small notebook that can remain in your
possession. Enjoy the weekend. It may well
change your life.

◆ ◆ ◆

Your thoughts and emotions are awhirl as you begin to comprehend the enormity of the experience unfolding before you.
You postpone understanding it all to a time when your pulse
and senses have quieted. As the Moderator has suggested, you
turn your attention to your young Guide.

The soulful eyes trigger an explosion of remembrances.
Having lost touch with much of this, you decide to write down
what you see. What strikes you most is the _____
_____ .

You extend an understanding hand as you recall the time

_____.

Holding the thought for a moment, it leads you to remember another time when _____

_____

_____.

You can't help but feel _____ and you're moved to say " _____

_____."

Your young Guide, sensing your objective, begins to help fill in some of the blanks, and volunteers "I sometimes feel

_____"

_____.

You feel a rush of affection as the honesty brings you back to that earlier time. You begin to remember how you _____

and how you _____

_____.

The remembrance has you caressing your young friend with a protective embrace. Your young self holds the embrace as you begin to release. Sensing the deep inner hunger, you tighten your hug and are filled to overflowing with a rush of tender, wordless communication.

After a moment of rebonding, your thoughts return to the Moderator's suggestion. The question is evident before it is even voiced. It is disarmingly simple, yet it is the granddaddy of all questions. Not wanting to disappoint the eager young face whose world is suddenly on hold pending your answer, you take your time. The question is "Who are we and where are we headed?"

In response to the first portion of the question, you reply softly, "We are _____

_____.

You assure the child you'll amplify your answer as the weekend unfolds. As for where you're headed, you find yourself quoting something you once read or heard, that "life is but a series of new beginnings" and that if the weekend goes according to your intuition, you believe that answer will be forthcoming soon, perhaps within a few hours. You both seem to spark to the prospect of the insights to come.

THE EPITAPH

With the understanding nod of a man who once sat in the audience, the Moderator gestures for the group's attention. He has two important points to make that he senses will help. The first has to do with the source of the learning to come.

"As our weekend progresses, you will likely learn many things. What you learn will be self-taught."

You find yourself admiring the peaceful confidence and focused presence of this engaging man. You listen even more intently. "The events of this weekend have been carefully constructed to put you back in touch with yourself. Enlightened and facilitated by those who have assembled here to help, your experiences will function as a sort of midwife in helping you to achieve the rebirth or self-renewal you desire. But, I say again, the core work and directional cues will come from you."

You came here in pursuit of rejuvenation and already you're aware of a difference. Instead of being pulled down by thoughts of self-doubt, you find your whole being is poised and ready for the challenge at hand. You sense the upturn has already begun.

"My second point is related to the first. While this weekend will serve as a jump-start push on your road to personal fulfillment, the agent of change remains yourself. You will be responsible for carrying forth what you learn here and for putting it into practice. You will receive, however, a farewell gift to assist you as your journey through life resumes; a gift which, like 'the road less traveled,' will make all the difference."

The group seems suspended in air, with a heightened sense of readiness. The Moderator, sensing his preparatory comments have been taken to heart, pushes ahead.

"Your first assignment will be to write a short epitaph for yourself. One to three sentences that you would like said about you on the occasion of your death."

The Moderator realizes the potential mood-dampening impact and the problem this exercise might pose for some. He offers some additional background. "Having been made in the image and likeness of God, as products of the Great Creator himself, we have each been born to create. Since all acts of creation start with a vision, it is fitting for us to begin at the end. By contemplating your mortality and the fact that your life will be subject to such a summary one day, why not write it yourself today. That way you'll have the rest of your life to devote to its accuracy."

His logic is impeccable and you're intrigued by the opportunity to prewrite history. As you reach for the pad and pencil, you caution yourself to take your time. You also find yourself nodding at the Moderator's final instruction to trust in your heart and not to worry, that the words will come.

With notebooks at the ready, a library-like silence blankets the group. After a few moments of deep reflection and boosted by the wide-eyed encouragement of your young Guide, you set to work.

Epitaph for _____ : _____

_____

_____

_____

Softly, you read aloud what you've written to your young Guide. You enjoy a moment of peace and reassurance.

Gradually the quiet is replaced with pockets of conversation as the writing ceases. The Moderator, looking at his watch, notes it is almost time to prepare for the evening's activities. First, however, he as an important point to make.

"At one time or another, we all have heard about people who, having lost one or more of their sensory faculties, develop compensating, heightened abilities in other areas. Someone like Helen Keller who, born without sight or hearing, developed unusual abilities and keen insights from her dark, silent, contemplative world.

What I'd like you to consider is what Helen Keller said when asked her perspective on life. After considerable reflection, she concluded 'life is either a daring adventure...or nothing.'"

The children are quick to respond to the excitement and intrigue of the front end of that rather broad continuum while the adults seem far more contemplative. The Moderator picks up on their introspection.

"Which is the case in your life now? Are you living in a way that is deeply satisfying to you, that allows you to give expression to your full range of interests and capabilities? Or are you marking time, waiting for your proverbial ship to come in or for some imagined, shadowy, big person, some surrogate parent, to rescue you in the eleventh hour and take charge of your life?"

While the adults are momentarily occupied mulling over their own satisfaction indices, the Moderator flips the top sheet of the nearby easel pad to reveal a large sketch of a rocking chair and a wheelbarrow. The children begin to stir en masse, perhaps questioning the connection between the two dissimilar objects. The speculation is short-lived.

"I have come to see anyone who marks time in a job, a career or in a relationship that has lost its zip, or perhaps never had it in the first place, as being the occupant of a rocking chair. It offers the occupant something to do at the moment but doesn't get him anyplace; doesn't help him to grow and to experience life at the preferred end of the Helen Keller description.

With the passage of time, the underlying lack of fulfillment and stimulation will take its toll, acting like a giant lid, slowly suffocating the bewildered hard worker below. If too much time elapses, we may be jolted awake one day, as life has a habit of doing, to find we're not only curled up in a rocking chair but we've turned into a wheelbarrow in the process...which, as you may know, is something that is useful only when pushed, and is easily upset."

The restrained laughter serves to further underscore the accuracy of his analogy. The Moderator pauses to allow the sharing to subside, catching a glimpse of his watch. He has an important point to make but first wishes to excuse the children. Due to the unique role each young Guide will be asked to play in the weekend, an evening of orientation and entertainment has been prepared for them. The senior contingent will be attending a small dinner party. You are told you and your Guide will have adjoining rooms at the neighboring Inn and will be reunited before retiring.

As the youngsters are led off, the Moderator is keen to return to his previous train of thought and gestures back to the easel drawings.

"While many of us may have succumbed to the 'should do' voices in our respective worlds, a large number opted to shun traditional roles altogether and to go in search of personal fulfillment elsewhere.

Richard Louv, a nationally syndicated and award-winning columnist with the San Diego Union, chronicled this migration in his book *America II*. A deep thinker and a futurist, Louv observed a wave of people who concluded 'you could change your inner environment by changing the external. You could try, with some potential for temporary success, to satiate a gnawing hunger. You could move.'[1]

In what he called 'an age of discontinuity,' Louv attributed the underlying motivation to 'a search for home.' He found when the word home is mentioned, it strikes deep, but it is a peculiar home that is pictured, 'one that exists as much in the future as in the past.'[2]

Louv further points out, 'a beautiful phrase, coined by demographer Peter A. Morrison, captures what seems always to have drawn Americans: *the image of elsewhere*. America, after all, was set up as an escape from the past. But that image seems just beyond their grasp.'[3]

Louv interviewed a number of transplants and had this observation: 'What they describe is the seductiveness of the image, how it makes us think again and again that the real American dream can be found somewhere else. There is so much in the society that pushes us consciously and unconsciously in this direction. But the final secret of *America II* is simple and discomforting. There isn't any place to hide.'[4]

The migration Louv described appears to be coming full circle. Researchers who monitor the public are finding more and more people are fed up with materialism. They're looking for more meaning. They want to feel more stable, more grounded than earlier periods when they shunned traditional roles and went in search of 'themselves.' The unsettled lives they chose proved — inevitably — unsettling.

What begins to take shape out of the haze is we each have to build meaning into our own lives. While many may start out expecting and wanting the magic to come from outside themselves, we all must eventually yield, some ever so slowly, to the fact it can only come from within us. It won't be easy to find happiness within ourselves, but experience has shown, after many side-road excursions, it's just not possible to find it elsewhere.

We're not ready to push for answers just yet, but it is time to reflect on the notion of commitment. Specifically, that we build meaning into our own lives, and we do it through our commitments.

Think about what your commitments are now or have been over the years. Have you in fact made any yet, or did you inherit or buy into someone else's view on what you should be doing with your life?

No decisions are needed at this point, just some good, old-fashioned reflection. While you're at it, think about whether your friends would categorize you as a complainer or a gainer. Again, no hard and fast decisions needed. Just something else to toss into the pot and let simmer for awhile."

You find your thoughts racing ahead, trying to anticipate what the next two days might hold. The thought of spending real quality time with your eight-year-old self is reason enough to feel uplifted. After conferring with one of the attendants, the Moderator has grown more animated, unable to contain his zeal for the activity ahead. A private banquet room has been reserved for a dinner party which you will host. This is to be a very special dinner party indeed.

The Moderator continues, "From all the people you have ever known, you may invite eight guests to join you for an evening of magnificent food, good cheer and inspired conversation. Since this is a magical Neighborhood, even those who have passed away may be invited."

You are instructed to make a list of your eight guests and to place their first names on a seating chart just handed you. The seats to your left and right are to be places of honor.

Your spirits are soaring at the prospect of such a get-together. You complete the list and seating chart with considerable deliberation.

<u>Dinner Party Guests:</u>

1. _____   5. _____

2. _____   6. _____

3. _____   7. _____

4. _____   8. _____

<u>Seating Diagram:</u>

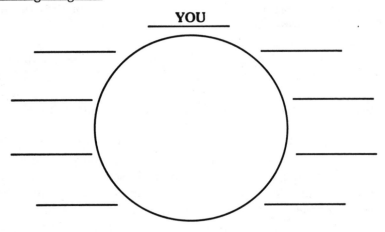

NOTES:
[1] Richard Louv, *America II*, (Los Angeles: J.P. Tarcher, 1983), p. 9.
[2] Ibid. p. 3.
[3] Ibid. p. 4.
[4] Ibid. p. 254.

Chapter 3

THE DINNER PARTY

You arrive at the banquet wing of the Inn, eager to begin, yet aware of some trepidation. While dressing you had begun to calculate some of the conversations to come, but something within you advised against it. Perhaps it was the Moderator's earlier advise to trust your heart, that the right words would come. You are relaxed and ready.

You are led down a corridor and the sound of merriment is evident from a number of nearby rooms. You enter your assigned room and are pleasantly surprised to find your guests are already seated and engaged in conversation. Your escort suggests you move around the table in a clockwise manner greeting each with a brief welcome and the promise of a long chat to follow. The escort advises you to take your notebook along to record whatever words, images or feelings are triggered at each of these brief reunions. A violinist will keep the group's attention while you make your greetings.

Thoughts about Guest 1 _____: _____
_____
_____
_____

Thoughts about Guest 2 _____: _____

_____

_____

_____

Thoughts about Guest 3 _____: _____

_____

_____

_____

Thoughts about Guest 4 _____: _____

_____

_____

_____

Thoughts about Guest 5 _____: _____

_____

_____

_____

Thoughts about Guest 6 _____: _____

_____

_____

_____

Thoughts about Guest 7 _____: _____

_____

_____

_____

Thoughts about Guest 8 _____: _____

_____

_____

_____

As you return to your seat, you gesture to the violinist to cease for a moment. It is time for a welcoming toast. With a broad smile and warmly scanning those present, you say

"_____

_____."

Instantly upon taking your seats, the food is served. In keeping with this unprecedented setting, everyone was instructed to order their dream meal. It is now placed before them. The room soon fills with raves of palatal pleasure and the clanking of silverware against fine china. As the last morsels are consumed, a mood of contentment seems to blanket the room.

It has been years since you've indulged yourself so thoroughly at the dinner table and you sense each of your guests has been similarly satisfied. As the violinist begins playing requests, your escort returns and suggests it is time to take each guest aside and speak to them from your heart, saying what perhaps has been muffled or withheld in the past. Many of these conversations are long overdue.

> Editor's Note: Take as much time as you need to develop your thoughts. Visualizing each guest in your mind's eye should help trigger what needs to be said.

You approach Guest 1 and are pleased to find the words do flow effortlessly.

Your comments for Guest 1 _____ : _____

_____

_____

_____

_____

Your comments for Guest 2 _____ : _____

_____

_____

_____

_____

Your comments for Guest 3 _____: _____

_____

_____

_____

_____

_____

Your comments for Guest 4 _____: _____

_____

_____

_____

_____

_____

Your comments for Guest 5 _____: _____

_____

_____

_____

_____

_____

Your comments for Guest 6 _____: _____

_____

_____

_____

_____

_____

Your comments for Guest 7 _____: _____

_____

_____

_____

_____

Your comments for Guest 8 _____: _____

_____

_____

_____

_____

♦ ♦ ♦

The evening has more than served its purpose.

As the last of your guests depart, your thoughts shift to your young Guide. You hurry back to your room hoping there's still time to do the tucking-in honors. You arrive just as the lights go off. The light from your own room provides ample illumination. As you approach the bed, the ear-to-ear grin tells you the night was a success for the youngsters as well. You sit on the edge of the bed and shake your head in disbelief. You're inclined to pinch yourself to see if you're dreaming but your young friend beats you to the punch. You wrestle playfully for a moment and in a flash you're eight-years old again. It's as if time were suspended and you're back in the eight-year-old body yourself. You re-experience the insecurities and fears, the worries about the future, how you're doing in school and the good moments as well. It all comes flooding back. One second you're the child in bed longing to be loved and appreciated, and in a blink you're back to your present self.

Slowly you stroke the young forehead, pushing back the tousled hair. Never before have you felt so certain about what you wanted to say. Kissing the freshly exposed forehead, your words are straight from the heart. With your eyes echoing the words, you say, " _____

_____

_____

_____

_____

_____

_____

_____."

You retire to your room to make sense of it all. Your heart is full to overflowing and your stomach is running a close second. This has been a special day indeed. You fall asleep thankful for your many blessings and wonder what could possibly be planned for the morrow that could top this.

Chapter 4

BREAKFAST — DAY ONE

You awaken to find your rooms open onto a small terrace overlooking a beautiful garden. A table for two has been set and breakfast will be served when you're ready. Time has been provided to accommodate your morning routine which might include going for a run or walk. Afterwards, you hurry through your shower, hungry to sample the delights of this glorious new day. The sun is shining, the air is warm and breakfast is about to be served.

As you occupy yourself with the breakfast menu, you look up to see your young Guide totally enthralled by the antics of a nearby squirrel. You become equally mesmerized, not with the squirrel but with your young self. How could the world have become so distracting that you lost touch with such moments? You find yourself lost in remembrances. You especially remember how _____

_____

_____

_____.

The memories are vivid and powerful. You decide what you're feeling must not get lost again. You pick up your pencil and write "I feel _____

_____

_____

_____

_____

_____."

    Like everything else in your weekend so far, you find the breakfast to be remarkably good; somehow just what your body needed. You feel rested, refreshed and ready.
    As the breakfast dishes are cleared, a small card is uncovered. It contains questions with space for a brief answer and a reminder about the morning agenda.

Question #1. Are you pleased with your weekend experience to this point?
You reply," _____

_____

_____."

Question #2. What most sticks out in your mind? Any surprising insights so far? After due reflection, you answer," _____

_____

_____."

Question #3. Do you have any pressing unfinished business you'd like to resolve here? This question requires a bit more deliberation. When you're ready, you write," _____

_____

_____."

**PLEASE REASSEMBLE ON THE GREEN
AFTER BREAKFAST**

The walk back to the Green pays an unexpected dividend. You overhear a young girl behind you giggling and turn to find you are the center of the fun. It seems you have been stepping on many of the sidewalk cracks and the count is up to seven. Your young Guide figures it out and clues you in as you all share a good laugh.

You try to remember the last time you had occasion to consciously step over the cracks. While you're thinking, you find yourself extending your gait to avoid additional contact. You laugh at your own conformity and this unexpected lesson on the power of suggestion. You also pause to wonder what other staples of youth have dropped from your consciousness, or sadly, were never experienced.

The Moderator seems truly delighted to see everyone so upbeat and playful. He has the air of an expectant father who knows the glorious moment is close at hand. As the last few twosomes take their seats, the Moderator seems himself to be drawing energy and new vigor from the proceedings. He commands your attention as well as a growing curiosity and respect.

"Good morning to you all. I can tell by your faces and your focused attention the weekend is progressing nicely. We have a good bit of ground to cover today, but ample time will be provided for you both to continue to reconnect.

Let's get underway with a couple of stories. The first was told to me by a visiting priest who was giving the Sunday sermon at a former parish of mine. Although an older man, probably well into his seventies, I was taken by his vigor and evident strength of spirit. I was even more taken by his story.

An earlier experience had profoundly influenced his life and he wanted to share it. It was not so much a retelling as a poignant reliving. He brought us back in time to when he was fresh from the seminary, just 'one week' old as he phrased it. No doubt he was traveling back forty years or more, yet he spoke with a passion and such a detail-laced recall that it seemed as fresh as yesterday in his mind.

Having just arrived at his first parish assignment, he found himself alone in the rectory when the phone rang. Reluctantly he answered it, feeling suddenly unsure of himself. It was the local hospital calling. One of his parishioners, a woman, was dying from a respiratory illness.

Before the phone rang he had been reviewing some of his seminary notes. He had come across a quote from St. Thomas Aquinas that left him as unenlightened then as it had when he first read it years earlier. Aquinas had said, "Happiness is the conscious possession of a good." The phone call had interrupted this most recent attempt to grasp Aquinas' meaning.

The hospital spokesman said the woman was gravely ill and could he hurry over. As he hung up, he felt his anxiety grow. He had practiced the various liturgies untold times in the safety of the seminary, but this was different. This was for real.

He recalled flipping through his liturgy book in the car on the way to the hospital, boning up one last time. The memory seemed to yank him back to the present. He raised his head, smiled and with an air of embarrassment said, 'You know, I may well have made religious history that day. The bookmark had fallen out on the way and in my nervous confusion I may have opened to the wrong page. I may have inadvertently ordained the first woman priest that afternoon.'

The humor of such an unthinkable blunder rippled through the congregation. Then in an instant we were transported back to the hospital room. All his seminary practice could not have prepared him for what followed.

The woman was having trouble breathing. Each and every breath was a struggle. He quickly overcame his inconsequential nervousness when he comprehended the gravity of her condition.

The pain was so severe, she was passing in and out of consciousness. While conscious, she had but one thought, one desire. In spite of the pain, she retained a stoic dignity and repeatedly asked of God, 'Please, just one pain-free breath.'

That's all she wanted, one pain-free breath.

Such a simple request, being able to breathe freely. It is something we all take for granted, yet it had become the richest of all treasures now that it was not in her possession.

After watching helplessly for what seemed hours, he found himself doubting God's goodness, questioning how he could permit such a struggle. Each breath, a sheer act of courage in itself, was greeted and cruelly rewarded with more unbearable pain. She wanted desperately to live, but the battle had taken its toll. Her physical strength could not keep up with her will and strength of character. The priest listened to her last, labored breaths and then . . . the heroic struggle was over.

He sat perfectly still in the now quiet room. He was certain God was embracing her now, providing the comfort she sought so desperately in her final hours. He felt relief that her pain was over, but more than that, he felt an immense pride in the noble struggle he had witnessed. He also felt guilty about how freely he had always breathed, never once having given it a second's thought.

As he left the hospital, the crisp evening air was invigorating and helped focus his thoughts. He took in a deep breath; but, unlike a lifetime of earlier breaths, this one was special. This one he really owned.

He thought of that brave woman and of Aquinas' definition of happiness. 'The conscious possession of a good.' The elusive meaning was not only revealed, but the experience seemed to throw a master switch in his own consciousness. His whole being felt illuminated by the clarity of this fundamental of all insights. His life would never be the same.

Some forty years later, the experience was still burning bright in his heart. In a kind, fatherly way he suggested we reflect for a moment on the things we often allow to clutter our minds, diverting our precious consciousness in the process. He wasn't scolding so much as he was trying to impart the irony of it all. Here we all sat, each of us possessing that good — that ability — but none of us consciously possessing it in the manner Aquinas suggested. We get distracted by work or school pressures, marital or social stresses and the ever-present pile of bills.

Being fond of aphorisms, the old Chinese adage 'If you want to know the road ahead, ask those coming back' served to further heighten the poignancy of this visiting priest's message. Here was a seasoned life's traveler, sharing the moment in his lifetime that had touched him most profoundly. Much like a speaker will conclude a talk by identifying the one thing they hope you'll remember, this religious man had selected, from all his lessons and encounters, the one that continued to be the most meaningful and the most helpful in his life to date.

I can't speak for the rest of the congregation that morning, but I was moved by the power and the simplicity of the message. Although not profoundly new — remembering to 'count your blessings' is a frequently heard admonition — it had a new clarity that was unmistakably and unshakably dead center."

You glance down and notice your young Guide is thoughtfully taking it all in. You break a small smile and return your attention to the podium.

"As I reflect now on that priest's story, I realize how similar it is to the central message of Thornton Wilder's classic play *Our Town,* an equally arresting story of a young woman who dies in childbirth and is allowed to return to earth for one day. She chooses her twelfth birthday as the day she will relive. Upon returning, and to her horror, she finds everyone is too preoccupied with petty involvements to appreciate the grandeur and the splendor of each precious moment. After imploring her mother to really look and really listen 'while yet we may,' she recoils at the sad and rampant misuse of time on earth. Despondently, she asks to be taken back, calling out: 'Good-bye Momma, good-bye Pappa, good-bye Grovers Corners. Good-bye to clocks ticking, and to food and hot coffee...to freshly ironed dresses and hot baths...to sleeping and waking up. Oh earth, you're too wonderful for anyone to realize you.'

As the play closes, she asks the stage manager whether anyone on earth ever appreciates life while they have it 'every, every minute.'

'No,' he replies, 'maybe the poets and the saints, maybe they do some.'

The curtain falls on her final sad words of resignation: 'That's all human beings are, blind people.'

It's a moving story. Many of us could benefit by periodically recalling the young woman's impassioned plea 'Momma, Pappa, let's look at one another while yet we may.'"

You find yourself nodding and questioning how often you too have succumbed to this figurative blindness. As your eyes meet your young Guide's, you are heartened by the thought that whatever your track record in the past, the future will now be different. This weekend is seeing to that.

The Moderator seems to be energized by his own words. You feel drawn by his natural enthusiasm for the subject matter. You share his eagerness to continue.

"This next story I first came upon while reading Denis Waitley's self-help book *Seeds of Greatness* a number of years ago. As Denis tells it, he was going through an introspective period in his life, having just survived a life-threatening boating accident. It was one of those 'jolts' we all receive in life that prompts us to take stock; to step back and look with a penetrating, laser-beam intensity at the most recent collection of habits and involvements we now call our life.

Typically, during these periods of reassessment, this weekend being a prime example, we become open for advice and inspiration. Denis Waitley found it in the title selection from a collection of Loren Eiseley essays entitled *The Star Thrower*. Upon reading the essay myself, I found Denis' interpretation triggering a few of my own. What follows then is a blended interpretation, with full credit to Denis for having led the way.

The Star Thrower is the story of a middle-aged man who travels to the shore to reflect on his life. His mother had recently died and he was questioning the meaning of it all. Early one morning, after a rather severe evening storm, he arose early and headed off for a walk. The storm and evening tide had left a new bounty of sea shells strewn along the beach.

It was tourist season, and a race was on to see who could accumulate the choicest and most exotic shells. But on this particular morning, the man was not part of the frenzied race. He viewed it with a detached aloofness. He was in search of something far more valuable and far more elusive. He was looking for himself.

After watching the insensitive antics of what seemed to be the whole world out scrambling to get their share of shells, he became aware of a solitary figure further down the beach who was doing something odd. Instead of collecting, he seemed to be throwing what he found back into the sea.

The man moved in for a closer look. He was beyond curious, yet unaware he was closing in on the meaning that had eluded him for so long.

He watched the figure stoop to inspect something in the sand. He was almost upon him when the man slowly arose and flung the object out beyond the nearby reef. Before he could stifle his curiosity, he asked what the man was doing.

The answer was swift and simple. The evening tide had washed ashore and stranded a number of starfish. He was throwing them back out to sea so they could live. Yes, he answered, he was a collector of sorts, but 'only like this...only for the living.'

For Denis, the story was like finding the last piece to the puzzle of his life. The secret, he concluded, was 'to turn a life of collection into a life of celebration.'[1] It's your perspective — how you see life from within — that ultimately makes all the difference, that frees you to live in the moment.

This attitude, this perspective on life is easy to describe. I call it 'looking for the GOOD.' It entails getting to a place in our lives where we become creatively alive in the moment, remembering to look for the good in others, in ourselves, and particularly in each and every moment.

Yet, as we all learn, knowing where we want to go and getting there can be two separate and distinctly different challenges. Even for those who have sniffed out the right direction, we inevitably encounter obstacles along the way. Perhaps your obstacles take the form of an unfulfilling job or marriage, or you can't get motivated, aren't sure what you want, or, on a more basic level, have lost touch with who you are. Whatever your circumstances, the balance of the weekend will help draw out, from deep within you, the answers that have always been there. First, let's take a fifteen-minute break and give the youngsters a chance to romp a bit."

NOTE:
[1] Denis Waitley, *Seeds of Greatness*, (Old Tappan, N.J.: Fleming H. Revell Co., 1983), p. 218.

Chapter 5 ────────────

GOING WITH THE FLOW

The opportunity to stretch our legs felt good. The kids are once again focused, having worked off their restlessness. Everyone is seated and ready to resume as the Moderator flips a sheet of the pad resting on the easel to reveal this segment's topic — GOING WITH THE FLOW — KNOWING YOUR MOTIVATIONAL PATTERN.

The topic is dangerously close to that granddaddy of all questions you tap danced around yesterday. Your pulse quickens at the thought of shedding some new light on the subject.

After a few housekeeping details and an impromptu sharing of experiences to date, the Moderator focuses everyone's attention on the pad.

"Perhaps the best place to begin this discussion is at the very beginning — the Book of Genesis." The Moderator proceeds to describe the creation of the universe, reminding everyone God made them in His own image and likeness; that when He had created the world and man, He surveyed what He had made and He was pleased.

"The fundamental truth we need to grasp is that God created only GOOD — He wasn't in the habit of making junk — and that we have each been created 'to grow in wisdom, age and grace.' Your self-selection to attend this Weekend suggests you are progressing nicely on this intended growth path."

Pointing to the pad, the Moderator continues, "We are each like a river. The particular gifts and personality characteristics we are born with establish the flow of that river. If we choose careers and involvements in keeping with that flow, our lives will be filled with meaningful achievement, energy and inner peace. If we choose well — which is God's plan for us — our whole being will tell us we're on the right course. If we misread our flow, or never attempt to gauge it in the first place, life can become a tedious series of energy-zapping frustrations and disappointments."

The audience seems to choose the same moment to shift in their seats, applying this wisdom to their own lives. You can't help but wonder how many of the group are struggling with "rocking chair" jobs and involvements. You wonder the same about yourself. You give a confident nod to your young Guide that this is just what the doctor ordered. This is why you're here.

The Moderator flips the page on the easel to reveal the word ACHIEVEMENTS.

"In a moment I'll be asking you to make a short list of your major achievements. Things that you did well and felt good about at the time."

He takes a moment to explain why. "We are each born with a preset pattern, style and set of motivations. They begin to emerge in childhood and remain consistent throughout our lives. No matter what jobs or involvements we fall into, our inherent motivational pattern will influence how we define our role and where we place our emphasis. Our pattern will express itself in an indelible way in the achievements we are most proud of. As you'll see in a moment, buried in your past is a trail of evidence which indicates (he flips the easel sheet to reveal a series of points):

◆ whether you prefer working alone or with a team

◆ how you are energized (going within yourself or involvement with other people)

◆ a preference for subject matter (words, numbers, concepts personal relationships, designs, machines)

◆ a specific group of functional abilities (develop, organize, persuade, analyze, control, plan, execute)

◆ recurring circumstances (problems, projects, deadlines, competition)

◆ one main motivational thrust (build, get results, get recognition, acquire, discover, clarify, pioneer, serve, improve)

◆ how you gather information (focus on details or the big picture)

◆ how you make decisions

If you haven't already sniffed out your pattern, we will do so the balance of this morning. Why? Because a person experiences more and more fulfillment in life as he or she conforms to what he or she was created to become.

There is an additional reason 'to go with the flow' and that is to draw closer to your Higher Power. As Martin Buber described it, 'You'll find Him (the Eternal Thou) — Him who cannot be sought — by going out with your whole being to meet your Thou. It is a finding without a seeking.'[1] In other words, by being true to ourselves and by investing ourselves in the pursuit and development of our unique gifts, we move closer to the Ultimate Creator. By participating in an act of creation ourselves, as we 'take away the stone' and help to create our own lives, we pay honor and respect to the Ultimate Creator Himself."

The Moderator proceeds to allay any concerns that the exercises to come are difficult or tedious. "Contrary to what you might be thinking, the process is easy and actually fun. You start by listing what you feel are your six most noteworthy achievements. They may come from your work, family, personal life, schooling or leisure activities. Since we best reveal ourselves in our work, I suggest you start there. Please open your notebook to the tabbed section in the back and begin.

Your young Guide will make sure your early achievements are considered for inclusion. Once you've listed six achievements, go back and describe as best you can exactly what you did on each, how you did it, why and with whom. The more detail you can supply, the more productive and revealing our subsequent analysis will be. Remember, list the six first then go back and provide the detail."

As you reach for the notebook, your young Guide happily mentions a few of your early accomplishments. You write them down for possible consideration. You smile as those special memories are brought forward. They are:

1) _____

2) _____

3) _____

You turn to the tabbed section of the notebook, place it in your lap and contemplate the assignment. Certain achievements come quickly to mind. You decide to begin with those, certain that others will surface in due time. Under the wide-eyed stare of your young Guide, you make the following entries:

Accomplishment #1 _____

Description: _____

_____

Accomplishment #2 _____

Description _____

_____

_____

Accomplishment #3 _____

_____

Description: _____
                _____
                _____
                _____

Accomplishment #4 _____

Description: _____
                _____
                _____

Accomplishment #5 _____

Description: _____
                _____
                _____

Accomplishment #6 _____

Description: _____
                _____
                _____

You find your young partner's inquisitiveness very helpful in dredging up the supporting facts and details. After satisfying this almost palpable curiosity, you record the memories so activated.

As the sound of writing quiets, the Moderator presents the instructions for part two of the analysis. "This is where we begin to play detective. Go back and read through the achievement descriptions and circle all the verbs that indicate the action taken. (Past and current resumes are also good sources for these verbs). Once your verbs are identified and circled, we'll then group them by category." Once again he flips the easel sheet over, revealing:

ABILITY CATEGORIES

❑ Visualizing	❑ Implementing
❑ Formulating	❑ Constructing
❑ Planning	❑ Operating
❑ Creating	❑ Counseling
❑ Organizing	❑ Influencing
❑ Developing	❑ Supervising
❑ Investigating	❑ Teaching
❑ Evaluating	❑ Writing
❑ Learning	❑ Performing

You'll likely find your abilities centering in five or six areas. We're only interested here in verbs or abilities that have recurred over time. You'll find this same list of ability categories in the back of your notebook. After you've circled all your verbs, decide which category each comes closest to and put a check mark there. Once all your verbs are so categorized, count up the check marks. Those with two or more are your stronger abilities. In effect, they keep rising to the surface."

The care the Moderator is taking with this exercise further underscores its importance. You happily relinquish the pencil to your young partner and together have no problem zeroing in on the verbs. The classification stage takes a bit more time and discussion, with your young Guide eagerly awaiting the category decision and confidently recording each check mark. You make a good team.

> Editor's Note: Complete the verb analysis now. Enter your check marks above.

The moderator resumes his instruction and indicates your detective work is not yet complete. "Now let's move on to the 'nouns' — the words that describe the kinds of objects and mechanisms you gravitate to and are motivated to work with or upon. They also are descriptive of the circumstances or situations within which you seem motivated to work. As with the verbs, we're only interested in those that recur, that are suggestive of a pattern of attraction or interest. Now go back through your six accomplishments (resume too if available) and draw a box around all such nouns. Then tabulate how frequently each appears. Record your findings in the appropriate section in the back of your notebook" (see following):

Prevalent Objects/Subject Matter
(e.g., people, animals, words,
numbers, projects, hardware)   Frequency

❏

❏

❏

Prevalent Circumstances
(e.g., new, cause, productivity,
competition, trouble)   Frequency

❏

❏

❏

The Moderator congratulates everyone for the evident industry being devoted to the exercises. To keep everyone's concentration keen, he suggests going for a short walk. Sensing the younger members are a bit antsy, he points to a cart containing balls and toys of various sorts. Within moments the stampede is on. You watch as your young Guide _____

_____

_____

You feel _____

_____

You decide on the spot that in the future you will _____

_____

_____

_____

◆ ◆ ◆

When the break is over, the group seems reinvigorated and ready to resume. The Moderator calls the group to order and focuses attention on the easel pad which has been advanced to a sheet entitled "Your Central Motivation." The same information is listed in the back of your notebook. It reads:

YOUR CENTRAL MOTIVATION

❑ Develop/Build   ❑ Serve People/Cause
❑ Improve   ❑ Perfect a Skill
❑ Command   ❑ Fulfill Expectation
❑ Exploit   ❑ Qualify/Achieve Standard
❑ Gain Recognition   ❑ Acquire
❑ Influence   ❑ Prevail/Persevere
❑ Organize   ❑ Fix
❑ Manage   ❑ Pioneer

"The last investigative leg is to go back through your six achievements and characterize and label each according to the above list of central motivations. The motivation with the most entries is likely your central motivation."

You smile broadly as your young Guide commandeers the pencil and is ready to begin. You observe that children really do enjoy being of help and feeling important. You decide to remember that. Perhaps that's when adults first acquire their own appetite and need for same. You turn back to your achievement listing and begin to classify each. You record your findings below:

Achievement   Central Motivation

1   _____
2   _____
3   _____
4   _____
5   _____
6   _____

Once your central motivation assignments are made, you're ready to assemble your pattern into summary form. The last page of the tabbed section is where you assemble the pieces. It reads:

My central motivation is to _____.
My abilities are _____, _____ and
_____.
Relative to others, I work best_____.
My preferred subject matter is _____and
_____.
Prevalent circumstances for me are _____and
_____.

The Moderator is back at the podium. He seems very deliberate and purposeful in his manner. The group quiets out of respect to his authoritative presence. You sense some important information is to follow.

"We have been spending the morning reviewing and classifying history — your personal history, your achievements — for the purpose of identifying your motivational pattern. We have done this to help you understand yourself a little bit better; to understand that God blessed you with a certain mix of talents and traits and that it is the natural order of things for these traits to manifest themselves, to rise to the surface, to reveal themselves."

The Moderator pauses for a sip of water. You feel a growing admiration and friendship for this engaging man.

"Those of us who grew up owning our feelings and listening to our inner applause meter early in life will find these exercises confirm what they've known all along. But those of us who, for one reason or another, have not been in full touch with our feelings will find these exercises both revealing and thought-provoking. If you're in the later category, the next exercise should prove helpful. What you might call a career audit, the chart we'll be developing will help you assess your current job satisfaction and job compatibility relative to the ideal position for you. Other positions or careers you have under consideration can be arrayed as well."

He advances the pad to reveal a sample "Career Appraisal Form." (Figure 1.) He excuses those for whom career is not a concern or an issue, inviting them to enjoy some free time prior to lunch. Only a few twosomes opt for the free time. The Moderator smiles softly, somehow knowing that would be the case.

Editor's Note: If career is not an issue for you, proceed to page 171.

Standing astride the pad, he proceeds to orient the group to the components of the chart. "What you see here is a hypothetical example of someone much like yourself. He was unsure if his current job was right for him, so he took some time, just as you will in a minute, to elevate the review from an emotional plane to an analytical one.

As you can see, this person listed nineteen different job characteristics or personal strengths he thought relevant. When scoring how important each would be in his 'ideal position,' nine were judged to be extremely important. They were weighted as 10s on a scale of 1-10.

The value of the chart becomes evident as you move across the remaining columns. This individual's current job is just not ringing the bell. It indexes at 63 relative to the hypothetical 'ideal.' Not surprisingly, the indicated action is to begin looking around. Since the future of the current position shows possible improvement, from a score of 103 up to 131, this individual is advised to meet with his or her superiors before accepting a new job. In effect, find out how likely that improved scenario is before you arbitrarily cut bait. Of the four alternative jobs under consideration, option "C" should be pursued as a strong #1 priority. In fact, on paper it appears to be the ideal job for this individual, indexing at 99 relative to the hypothetical 'ideal.'

You'll find the chart as easy to construct as it is valuable to consult. It will help you understand why you like or dislike your current job and can help focus your energies if a range of jobs or career choices are in your mind. Once constructed, it can be a valuable reference tool you may want to consult should your contentment level slip in the future.

FIGURE 1
Career Appraisal Form
(Scale: 1-10, Not important to Extremely Important)

Job Characteristics	Your Ideal Position	Current Position Now	Current Position In 5 Yrs.	A	B	C	D
Challenge	10	8	9	8	9	10	7
Interesting Subj.Matter	8	8	8	8	9	10	5
Stimulating Boss/ Co Worker	10	4	6	6	8	0	6
Authority/Latitude	10	6	8	8	10	10	7
Compensation	9	6	8	8	7	10	4
Equity Ownership	6	0	0	0	6	10	0
Geographic Location	8	6	6	6	7	10	8
Training Program	6	4	4	4	6	6	2
Title/Prestige	10	5	8	9	10	10	8
Work Environment	8	6	8	7	6	10	7
Travel	6	6	6	6	2	2	6
Job Perks	7	2	4	2	5	10	0
Recognition	10	4	8	7	9	10	5
Career Path	10	6	8	7	7	10	5
Motivational Pattern:							
Oral & Written Skills	10	8	8	8	10	10	6
Inspiring/Teaching	10	6	8	10	10	10	5
Analytical Problem Solving	7	8	8	6	7	6	8
Strategic & Conceptual	8	6	8	6	8	8	8
Enhance Self-Esteem	10	4	8	8	10	10	5
Total	163	103	131	124	146	162	102
Satisfaction/ Compatibility Index	100	63	80	76	89	99	63

Assessment/Indicated Action:

♦ Not acceptable
♦ Begin to explore options

♦ Since future could be better, meet with superiors prior to accepting new position

♦ Pursue "C" as #1 priority

We have a few minutes before we break for lunch so please turn to the blank 'Career Appraisal Form' in your notebook. Feel free to use as many of the job characteristics from our example that are relevant for you. Be sure to add the special abilities and circumstances from your Motivational Pattern."

A warm smile consumes his face as he scans the group and adds, "Remember, there's a young mathematician at your side who can record your weightings and help with the tabulations once you get it set up."

You had gotten so engrossed in the discussion you missed the rather bored, detached look that seems to have contagiously spread amongst the youngsters. You reflect on the adult nature of the tedious-looking chart and you take a moment to thank your young Guide for being patient and for being such a special person. As you watch the young face light up in response to your words and touch, you make a note to remember this simple truth: take time to recognize and reinforce the GOOD around you, and be loving, nurturing and understanding, especially to your own inner child.

One last hug and playful pat and you jump into the assignment. Between the job characteristics from the sample, a few of your own, and your Motivational Pattern, the chart fills up quickly (refer to Figure 2 on page 169).

Editor's Note: Complete the chart one column at a time. After listing all relevant job characteristics and personal strengths in column 1, go back and weight each on a scale of 1 to 10 measuring just how important that characteristic or trait would be to you in an ideal job setting. Enter your weights in column 2. Moving to columns 3 and 4, and using the same 10-point scale, grade how well your current job measures up on each characteristic both now and how you project it to be in five years. Enter those gradings in columns 3 or 4. Do the same for any new job or career you might be contemplating. Label each column accordingly and enter your respective gradings. When done, you may find a pocket calculator helpful to total the columns and calculate the respective Compatibility Indices. The Index for each column is produced by dividing that columns total by the total from column 2. The Indicated Actions section will flow directly from the numbers and your heart. Take as much time as you need.

FIGURE 2
Career Appraisal Form

1	2	3	4	5	6	7
	Your			Jobs/Careers		
Job Characteristics/	Ideal	Current Position		Under Consideration		
Personal Strengths	Position	Now	In 5 Yrs.	___	___	___
_____	____	____	____	____	____	____
_____	____	____	____	____	____	____
_____	____	____	____	____	____	____
_____	____	____	____	____	____	____
_____	____	____	____	____	____	____
_____	____	____	____	____	____	____
_____	____	____	____	____	____	____
_____	____	____	____	____	____	____
_____	____	____	____	____	____	____
_____	____	____	____	____	____	____
_____	____	____	____	____	____	____
_____	____	____	____	____	____	____
_____	____	____	____	____	____	____
_____	____	____	____	____	____	____
_____	____	____	____	____	____	____
_____	____	____	____	____	____	____
_____	____	____	____	____	____	____
_____	____	____	____	____	____	____
_____	____	____	____	____	____	____
Total	___ (A)	(B)	___ (C)	(D)	(E)	(F)
Compatibility Index	(A)	(B)	(C)	(D)	(E)	(F)
	100 (A)	(A)	(A)	(A)	(A)	(A)
Assessment/Indicated Action:						

NOTE:
[1] Martin Buber, *I and Thou*, (New York: Charles Scribner's Sons, 1958), p. 11.

Chapter 6

THE MEADOW

What a glorious idea. A picnic lunch has been packed and a large block of time has been set aside. Your assignment is to just kick back in a nearby meadow and enjoy each other's company. With notebook in one hand and picnic basket in the other, you head down the assigned path having been assured your private meadow is only a five-minute walk away. Your young Guide is happily occupied carrying the blanket and a frisbee.

While there are no sidewalk cracks to avoid, you find a spring returning to your step as you walk deeper into the woods. It's as if layer after layer of calcified life experience were being striped away. What the mist failed to dissolve upon your arrival, this walk seems to be finishing. You feel absolutely wonderful. At one point you find yourself skipping, much to the delight of your young companion.

As you emerge from the woods, you are overcome by the natural beauty of the storybook meadow. Wild flowers abound and a gentle, warm breeze causes the unspoiled meadow grass to bend and sway in hypnotic waves. You find the perfect spot and spread the blanket.

Before you can open the basket, the frisbee is airborne. After much frolicking, and by the time the frisbee has visited much of the meadow, it mercifully lands on the blanket. You're ready to come in for a landing yourself, having amassed quite an appetite.

As your young friend begins to shadow a nearby butterfly, you begin to sample the delights of the picnic basket. You're not surprised to find they've thought of everything. The serenity of the setting and the ampleness of the food has you marveling at this continued good fortune. How could this all be?

You lie on your back and let the peacefulness of the moment touch every corner of your being. With sleep just a nod away, you are revived by your young partner's discovery of an instruction card under the dessert container. You prop yourself on one elbow and read the card aloud:

"Welcome back to nature. It's been here all these years awaiting your return. As you contemplate its many wonders and lie upon the earth, use this time to get back in touch with your roots. Reflect back on the years you lived with your parents.

To help pull them and that time into your consciousness now, lie down and close your eyes. When your body is comfortable and fully relaxed, picture your mother and father running through just such a springtime meadow as you now inhabit. The value of this picture will quickly become evident. It will speak volumes about their respective capacities for joy and their openness to each other, to nature and to others. Keep your notebook at the ready to record what you see."

You have a long talk with your young Guide about your parents. The discussion serves as a good primer for the exercise ahead. You stretch back out and let your entire body go limp. After a few restful moments, you begin to picture in your mind a beautiful meadow. You look about for your parents but to no avail. Then, from afar you see them moving forward. Their movement seems to be in slow motion. You observe the action for a full minute or two and are struck by what you see.

The most striking thing about them is _____
_____
_____.

This prompts you to think _____
_____
_____.

You focus for a moment on your mother. You remember that your mother was _____
_____
_____.

As you think about that, you feel _____
_____
_____.

Watching your father come across the meadow has reminded you that he was _____
_____
_____.

As you recall this, you feel _____
_____.

You're not sure what influence they had on you, but maybe
_____
_____
_____.

As the image of your parents in the meadow fades, you realize what you want to remember about your father is that he
_____
_____.

What you want to remember about your mother is that she

_____

_____.

Finally, what you want to remember about them as a couple is that they _____

_____.

You feel peaceful and accepting of these reflections and understandings. But your serenity is short-lived. Your young Guide returns from the latest butterfly chase echoing the instruction card to return to the Green when the visualization exercise is completed. After a few tosses of the frisbee, you pack up and head back. Instinctively you pause at the perimeter of the woods for one last glimpse of your meadow. Sensing an opportunity, you take a mental photograph, etching both the natural beauty and its calming tranquility into your mind for future reference.

You are heartened by the experience, somehow knowing you may have just made a new lifelong friend. Could this be the special gift the Moderator had mentioned earlier?

Chapter 7

AFTERNOON PROGRAM
— DAY ONE

The Moderator watches as everyone reassembles on the Green, evidently refreshed from their respective meadow experiences. The morning program had been intensive and the restful picnic setting was intended to be restorative. You feel wonderful and can't imagine ever feeling otherwise.

You marvel at the Moderator's sustained enthusiasm. His fatherly manner is both reassuring and authoritative. His every move suggests there is no other place he would rather be than standing on that podium at this moment. Everyone quiets as he begins to speak:

"It is safe to assume, from a quick survey of the returned picnic baskets, that lunch was enjoyed, if not a smashing success. Your Higher Power intended this to be a special weekend from front to back. Certainly the events so far would so indicate.

This afternoon's program is divided into two parts. The first portion we'll do as a group — a number of short exercises — and the balance of the afternoon will be up to you. A series of break-out sessions are available should you have some unfinished business to resolve or a relationship or marriage crisis to deal with. Should neither be the case, you'll have some free time to continue your enjoyment of these lovely grounds. You'll be guided as we go along."

The sun is high in the sky and although the group is blanketed in the shade of an immense old tree, you find yourself basking in a shaft of sunlight that has targeted the right side of your face. The warmth seems to be reaching down to the depths of your soul. You take a moment and thank your Higher Power for guiding you to this life-enhancing experience. Life is good at the moment and you wish to acknowledge that fact.

The Moderator continues:

"Considering the irrefutable logic we will excel more at the things we enjoy and feel strongly about, write down a short list of things that stir your passions — those subjects, ideas or activities that ring your bell; that when mentioned, discussed or participated in, cause your pulse to quicken and your interest and enthusiasm to soar. I think you know what I mean."

Your young Guide knows immediately and announces:

- ◆ _____
- ◆ _____
- ◆ _____

You contemplate your answer. When the time comes, you know instinctively what to say. You write:

- ◆ _____
- ◆ _____
- ◆ _____

The Moderator's next question is quite straightforward. "Do you have a dream or some distant calling?" You think for a moment then reply," _____
_____."

"On a related front, where do you go when you daydream and where do your prevalent conversations tend to go?"

Taking them in order, you reply, "When I daydream I find myself _____."

Continuing your answer, "I find my prevalent conversations tend to _____

_____."

As you reflect on these answers, you feel _____

_____

_____.

You look up to see the Moderator has written the word "TIME" on the large pad. He explains that how we view and use our time tells a lot about us. He then asks, "In the context of your own life, please define 'time.'" You're aware of a range of possibilities but decide on the following. You write, "Time to me is _____

_____."

Your answer awakens some additional thoughts. You find yourself sensing a breakthrough may be imminent. The Moderator continues, "Let's talk for a minute about what Ivan Pavlov, the Russian physiologist, stated on his deathbed when asked his advice for a successful life. Two words summed up this learned man's response...'passion and gradualness.'

A moment ago we attended to the passion component. Let's address now what Pavlov likely meant by 'gradualness.' One possible interpretation is to sit tight and wait for your ship to come in. I think you know Pavlov meant no such thing. In the context of committing to a goal, a goal you feel passionately about, Pavlov understood that such quests take time. Rather than impose an unrealistically tight schedule, a schedule destined to trigger disappointment and feelings of failure, Pavlov's counsel was to allow ample time; time to plan, implement and revise and time to allow your thoughts and energies to decant and evolve.

Someone once said, 'the fruits of success ripen slowly.' If Pavlov were here today, I'm sure he'd advise you to begin by targeting one of your passions and to stalk it with a gradual persistence. A persistence that would enable you to prevail against all obstacles...to strive, to persevere and to achieve.

This next exercise should help you put aside the rhetoric and assess how well you're managing your time. I apologize for any discomfort this may cause but the point is important. YOU HAVE JUST LEARNED YOU HAVE ONLY SIX MONTHS TO LIVE. Accept for the moment that your financial and legal affairs are in order. The question before you is how would you spend your last six months on earth?"

The flip answer you might have given in the past seems out of place. The spirit of the session demands a thoughtful answer. You find your eyes moving skyward as you begin to formulate a reply. Slowly, with a growing confidence, you write,"

_____

_____

_____ "

_____.

You instinctively realize the importance of what you've written, or just acknowledged to yourself. You find yourself scanning how you now spend your time as the Moderator suggests doing just that. He has advanced the pad to a page entitled "Time Audit." He suggests you take a few minutes and estimate how you currently spend an average week. You review the various categories, then make your entries:

Time Audit (Weekly)

Activity	Now	Percentage of Time 6 Months To Live
Family	___%	___%
Career	___%	___%
Spiritual	___%	___%
Friends	___%	___%
Community	___%	___%
Exercise	___%	___%
Mental Nourishment	___%	___%
Total	100%	100%

The Moderator has an important point to make. "Do not misconstrue the intent here. I am not promoting wholesale revolt and anarchy. I am simply using the extreme to make a point. It is human nature to wait, often until life hands us a jolt, before we awaken from our sleep walk. The hope is you will benefit from this simulated jolt without having to experience the real thing.

As you compare the two columns in your time audit, understand that any inconsistencies do not need to be realigned overnight or by next Thursday. The purpose is to get you to be more time sensitive, more aware of what is really important to you and more inclined to live your preferences now — to open up space in your life for them to happen now and to begin a program of self-conditioning to gradually become what you are sensing you were created to be."

The Moderator falls silent for a moment, looking for the words that will best launch his next topic. Your admiration for this remarkable man grows as you watch him work. His work is more a labor of love, his affection for the subject etched in every crease of his engaging, weathered face.

The elusive phrasing now grasped, the Moderator confidently strides to the easel and writes the words — A Standard of Stewardship. Before he finishes writing, he begins to speak.

"One of the most important duties of a parent, and perhaps the most susceptible to mishandling and parental contamination, is that of instilling in each and every child a sense of how truly unique and special they are as individuals. Unfortunately in America today, there is growing evidence as many as one in four children are being raised in dysfunctional households, where one or both parents are not there for them emotionally.

Children reared in such settings never learn to love themselves. Their parents are too absorbed in their own unresolved conflicts, compulsions and addictions to provide the nurturing, stroking and continual reassurance that the young child needs. When viewed against this backdrop of emotional neglect, it's not surprising that many of our young people are succumbing to substance abuse, falling behind in school and experimenting too soon with sex. The closeness and sense of relatedness and attachment that they hunger for cannot be found in drugs, alcohol or promiscuity. Whatever relief they do find is fleeting. The outgrowths of their discomfort — the distance and the loneliness — are not touched by these misguided, short-term fixes. The underlying feeling of inadequacy, and the fear and anxiety of not being loved and of not fitting in, return with a vengeance in the morning.

Children of dysfunctional families, not knowing what normal is, typically endure their pain in silence and without understanding they are not at fault. All the world seems to be operating just fine except for them. What makes the problem all the more insidious is that the deficiency is an emotional one and not likely to be diagnosed except in extreme cases. As a result, the person grows to adulthood and relies on their physical and intellectual maturity to sustain them, all the while struggling on the inside to find the identity and the validation they failed to get as a child. The search and the struggle can last a lifetime and, if not resolved, can be passed on to their children who inherit the same affliction — a nagging self-doubt born of low self-esteem and emotional immaturity."

This is a very sensitive subject and the group's rapt attention bears witness to its importance. The Moderator's gestures have compressed and his mood is increasingly solemn. He continues:

"Each and every baby born into the world is a miraculous gift from God. Stop by the nursery of your local hospital and watch the unbridled love and awe that parents of newborns feel, if you haven't already experienced those powerful feelings firsthand yourself. The late Jim Croce sang a haunting song about saving 'time in a bottle.' I'd like to borrow his concept and bottle up the surplus love and reverence for life that is so abundantly present at the time of birth and return it to each parent in measured doses on all ensuing birthdays until their child turns eighteen. A parent has no more important mission in life than to instill a sense of identity and specialness in each of his or her offspring.

The celebration of the new arrival should never end. The flame should burn brightly in the heart of the parents until it, in time, crosses over and is internalized by the child. Once the self-love candle is lit, it is a perpetual candle that will steadfastly emit its sustaining glow, flickering on despite inevitable buffeting from the winds of change.

Igniting the self-love candle in a child is a lengthy process. It's a function of time, attention and active listening. For parents with bright self-love candles of their own, the nurturing years come easy, serving to bolster and renew their own self-worth in the process. For parents whose candles were never properly ignited as children, the process will be a burden and a struggle. Unresolved resentments and the protective patterns of behavior learned in a dysfunctional upbringing can have damaging and disruptive consequences later. What suffers most is the frequency and the quality of the interaction time with their own children. Because of unresolved fears, anxieties and insecurities, the 'adult child' parents will often not show up emotionally for many of those small, seemingly inconsequential moments when their own children need to be hugged, listened to and made to feel special and important. The damage is cumulative and devastating, and worse, hardly ever diagnosed.

As gaps in a child's emotional foundation widen, the pull of peer pressure to fit in somewhere can be overpowering. Without a sense of self and internal values to fall back upon, many succumb to the temporary escape and false sense of connection they experience from drugs, alcohol or promiscuity. Can we blame them? They just want to feel comfortable and accepted, feelings they're denied at home."

For selected twosomes, the discussion seems to have touched a nerve. The Moderator pauses to allow the spontaneous sharing and comforting to subside. Then, with the bedside manner of a country doctor, he resumes:

"Parents teach their children primarily by what they do — not by what they say — and more and more our children are learning to self-medicate. At a time when the world should be their oyster, substance abuse and even relationship abuse can cloud their vision and fog over their minds.

Throughout the 1980s and now into the 90s, the subject of pollution control has captured many a headline. I support 100% the numerous efforts underway to preserve the quality of the environment for the generations to come. I have a bigger problem, however, with the pollution that is allowed to accumulate in the minds and psyches of people both young and old and that currently goes unmonitored. Indeed, let's talk pollution control, but let's begin the cleanup from the inside out.

As Walter Truett Anderson observed in his book *The Upstart Spring*, 'Perhaps there is something political in the human potential movement. Perhaps the humane society the civil rights activists and the peace protesters seek is to be reached by a long march through the psyche, through countless acts of personal transformation.'[1] Perhaps in a world increasingly alarmed by environment pollution, we need to spend equal time turning inward and addressing the internal pollution that might be continuing to contaminate our thoughts, our feelings and — most importantly — our self-image. If the violence and anger is to end, perhaps we need to remove it from our own hearts first."

Glancing momentarily at the easel, the Moderator continues: "What seems to have developed in our society is a book-end mentality towards life. We revere life at its inception, marveling at the miracle of birth and fussing over babies (correctly I might add). We also mourn life's passing, and are truly saddened by the finality and the magnitude of a lost life. Yet, we tend to allow the vast expanse of time in the middle to pass without imposing a 'standard of stewardship,' and without acknowledging the importance of individual self-esteem; without insisting on an institutionalized series of check points — self-esteem audits if you will — to ensure that each life traveler is equipped to experience and enjoy life to its fullest.

Inexplicably, the most important lessons in life, such as how to think and how to handle and manage one's feelings, are often left to each of us to sort through on our own. Without benefit of emotionally whole parents (in spite of best intentions) or grade school counselors trained to impart such knowledge, many of us are launched into adulthood without adequate preparation for the journey ahead. When the pressures of day-to-day living build, many succumb to self-defeating thoughts, debilitating bouts of depression or become vulnerable to drugs, alcohol or negative, addictive relationships."

Despite the serious tone and adult nature of the subject matter, the kids seem to understand. Your young self looks up with a halting, soulful expression. Instinctively you bend over for a hug. It's a deep, extended and bountiful hug. What you intended to be a gesture of reassurance suddenly blossoms into something much more. You feel the healing energy passing between you. What is unexpected is the healing going on deep within yourself. You hold the embrace, lost in the moment and oblivious to the restorative bonding that has swept the gathering.

A gleam returns to the Moderator's eyes. He ran a risk tampering with the mood of the group but the material prompted the connection he sought. He reminds everyone their weekend was structured to be just such a "march through the psyche," one of the countless singular acts of personal transformation that might in time transform the world.

Pockets of conversation erupt across the assembly and the Moderator wisely suggests the group take a five-minute break in place. Everyone is soon on their feet stretching out the kinks, a sight bearing a striking resemblance to the seventh-inning stretch at a ballgame.

NOTE:
[1] Walter Truett Anderson, *The Upstart Spring*, (Menlo Park, Ca.: Addison-Wesley, 1983), p. 291.

Chapter 8

CHANGE

The Moderator has used the break time to locate a couple of large signs. He carefully places them on the easel with their backs to the audience. You smile inwardly as you watch the curiosity grow amongst the younger set. The Moderator is similarly amused and opts to take advantage of their inquisitiveness.

"Your curiosity will be satisfied in a moment but first I have a question for you. Who can tell me what U. S. President's profile appears on the face of a penny?"

A chorus of "Lincoln's" erupts from the group, met by the Moderator's approving nod.

"You're quite correct, Abraham Lincoln. In time, you'll study about President Lincoln and his efforts to free the slaves. What you might not hear or fully appreciate is that Lincoln was also a student of human nature. His thoughts of liberation were not restricted to slavery alone.

He once observed that 'people are about as happy as they make up their minds to be.' There's a word lurking in the background of this seemingly innocent statement that many people are not prepared to accept. Yet, emotional freedom and peace of mind will remain forever beyond their grasp until it is acknowledged and heeded."

He walks over to the easel pad and announces as he writes: "That word is CHOICE."

Putting the magic marker down, he continues:

"Much has passed under the bridge since Lincoln so correctly pinpointed the problem. Significant advances in medicine, industrial technology and space exploration have dramatically changed the world and life as he knew it. Yet, the insightful words of Lincoln ring as true today as then, perhaps even more so.

If there's one moment in a person's life that marks the passage of youth into maturity — and I mean emotional rather than physical maturity — it would be that moment when we finally realize and *accept* that we each have to create our own world. This is not exactly what many of us want to hear. After years of investing ourselves in blaming others — in reciting chapter and verse why our lives have not fallen into place yet — to even entertain an alternate explanation, much less embrace it, would be too threatening, too much of a self-betrayal.

Paul Kurtz in his book *Exuberance — A Philosophy of Happiness* describes the sobering impact of this unalterable truth as follows: 'the destiny of man, of all men and of each man, is that he is condemned to invent what he will be — condemned if he is fearful but blessed if he welcomes the great adventure.'[1]

The breakthrough occurs when we finally comprehend and accept that what we become in life is our choice ... that we already are in fact what we have chosen to be so far."

The group is warming to the notion of responsibility and self-determination, but for some the needed acceptance will come reluctantly. The Moderator understands this and is prepared to address it.

"With only one life to live, it's time to recapture the sense of awe and specialness that surrounded your birth. It's time to begin to live like you really mean it. To get your heart into it. No matter how much time has elapsed in your life, our mission is to get out front and to lead the beautiful portion that remains. Dare I say there can be no more important matter on your plate at this time. None!"

The group seems to shift en masse in their seats, ready for the insights and exercises to come. The Moderator continues:

"Eventually we all come to realize our time on earth is the only important possession we have. Unfortunately, we live in an age where much of our time gets chewed up for us. A recent study by a time management expert confirmed most people spend little time on things they value...like their families. The study found the average person spends six months at stop lights, eight months opening junk mail, one year searching for lost objects, two years playing phone tag, four years doing housework, five years in line and six years eating."

The Moderator is too focused on making his point to pick up on the kids particular interest in the time study; namely, how much time gets "wasted" doing housework. In spite of their spirited speculation, the Moderator doesn't stray from his train of thought.

"Staying with this time perspective, life is just a progression of 'nows.' Unfortunately, many of us fail to live fully in the now. We rehash history and old hurts, or needlessly worry about the future and how we'll handle it. We do not come upon these tendencies by chance. How we think and behave, and how we manage our time, are learned habits...the result of conditioning.

We are each uniquely molded by our parents; the sum total of all the experiences and interactions during our early and formative years. Even the habit patterns we least admire in our parents, we often unconsciously learn to imitate. Fortunately these tapes can be overridden and replaced. We start by becoming more aware of how we think, feel and act."

The Moderator pauses to turn the first chart around on the easel, being careful to keep its various overlays in place. The visible part of the chart is depicted in Figure 3.

"As this Chart suggests, each of us is ultimately in pursuit of the same GOOD. We each want to love and be loved and to find a meaningful purpose in life; a purpose that will fill our days with energy — born of our accomplishments — and the peace of mind that flows from commitments freely made and earnestly pursued.

Having been made in God's image, man is at his core good. Much like our brethren further down the chart in the animal kingdom, we are biologically preset to mate and raise offspring. We do this in family units and in social groupings where compassion and love hopefully abound. I say hopefully, because as the chart suggests, on our way to getting in touch with the GOOD we often encounter obstacles (he removes the center drape - see Figure 4). Due to early childhood experiences, we may have inherited some emotional "not-okay" feelings that will need attention before we can begin to even see the GOOD, much less experience it as a steady diet. The obstacles blocking our path can and do vary widely, yet when reduced to their basics probably are being propelled by one or more of the culprit elements listed here. Whether readily identifiable as such or dressed up in new clothing, underneath virtually all the obstacles you might enumerate will likely be operating some combination of anger, resentment, misinterpretation and selfishness. The inevitable feelings of disappointment, frustration and deprivation that result, once triggered, can create a barrier and a blockage as strong as any prison wall.

The presence of such obstacles in our lives is more the rule than the exception. In spite of ups and downs, and at times more downs than ups, it does help to remember we have not been singled out for an especially harsh life. The Bible is clear that when Adam and Eve succumbed to temptation, all who followed would as a consequence be exposed to good and evil, joy and suffering.

What you're experiencing is what was planned for all of us. The world as we know it was designed to function as a stage. Albert Camus, the French philosopher and author, makes the point in *The Stranger* that we each need to eventually accept 'the benign indifference of the universe.' In effect, the stage we are launched upon at birth is just that — a stage; a stage we will occupy for an uncertain time, where we will be judged both for the quality of our performance *and* — listen carefully — the script we eventually write for ourselves."

The repeated emphasis of the elements of choice and personal responsibility is not lost on the group. The Moderator is pleased.

"Camus' observation of a 'benign indifference' in the universe is a key one. I interpret it as a viewpoint that God propped the stage with equal measures of good and evil. In other words, he set up a fair fight. But make no mistake about it, it was meant to be a fight...a struggle. Martin Luther perhaps said it best when he likened our time on earth to a personal passage through the Red Sea...that we are each put here and challenged to break free from our specific personal inheritance and bondage, much like the Israelites broke free from four hundred years of bondage in Egypt.

An old rabbinical expression states that a man enters life with his fist clenched but leaves with his hand open. Suggesting that we each have to progress from being shell collectors to being star throwers...to investing our thoughts and our time in looking for the GOOD and being creatively alive in the moment."

The Moderator moves to the left portion of the chart and removes the remaining drape (see Figure 5).

"We also learn in time there are certain tools we need to acquire to help us weather the normal ups and downs of life. As shown here, these tools are:

✓ positive self-esteem
✓ positive self-direction
✓ positive attitudes and beliefs

Now, the presence of obstacles in your life merely indicates you're alive, still on stage and that one or more of these essential tools needs some work. In many ways, I find that an exhilarating thought. You will too in time if you're not there already."

Setting the detailed chart aside, the Moderator uncovers two simplified versions.

"This chart (see Figure 6) is designed to show where many of us likely are right now. The obstacles have accumulated and aggregated over time and now block our ability to see or experience much of the GOOD in our lives. The final chart (see Figure 7) completes the picture of where we're heading. With the balance of your weekend devoted to obstacle removal or reduction, we'll be opening up numerous new channels or sight lines to help us both see and experience the GOOD on a steady basis."

The Moderator collects the various charts and passes them off stage. He apologizes to the kids for the rather adult nature of the recent topics and begs their continued indulgence. With that, he suggests the next topic warrants the group's undivided attention. After writing the word INTERPRETATIONS on the pad, he begins again:

"Our belief system — our attitudes and emotional view of the world — is at the root of all our thoughts, opinions, conversations and actions. It is our on-board computer scanner that drives all our interpretations. We are forever judging and interpreting events around us based on what we believe to be true in the world. The individual programs that instruct and guide this computer scanner are our attitudes. They are that central in our lives. If these attitudes and beliefs remain frozen and beyond examination, our growth will stagnate and our lives will become truly circular.

What we often fail to realize is how pervasive and dominating our attitudes become. Their hold over us is near tyrannical, and they manifest themselves in our preconceptions and predispositions. They influence how we see and hear the events around us. M. Scott Peck in his wonderful book *The Road Less Traveled* had this to say on the blinding influence of our preconceptions, 'Not until our perceptions are disengaged from the domination of our preconceptions are we free to experience the world as it is in itself.'[2]

No doubt Socrates had this very thing in mind when he said, 'The unexamined life is not worth living.' He, like Scott Peck, understood that the destroying circularity of a life must be broken by the person living it. That no one else can challenge and remove the attitudes that so control and dictate our behaviors. Only we can do this for ourselves.

An awareness of history begins to surface as a key element here. In this case, your own personal history and the unique chain of events that have contributed to who you are at this point in your growth. Kierkegaard had this sorted out years ago when he said 'Life can only be understood backwards, but it must be lived forwards.' In this context, I believe Kierkegaard was also issuing a caution. Like Socrates, he knew the importance of the backward glance as an aid in understanding and as a perspective enhancer. He also seemed to be warning us not to linger there or to drag the past forward into the present. But that's exactly what we do when we allow the unchallenged attitudes from our past to continue to trigger our thoughts, interpretations and conversations today.

Our attitudes are nothing more than recordings or mental imprints that established an early beachhead in our minds. The more we replayed them, the more entrenched they became and continue to become. Yet, their very existence and the air time they may have usurped in the past in no way implies they were accurate or valid thoughts then or now. They simply got a foothold in our minds before we had any conscious say in the matter. Things are different now. We are awakening to new choices. We need not remain captive to the thoughts of old.

If we do not challenge our beliefs and attitudes, as Socrates and others advise, we are abdicating to a past we likely had very little control over. Worse, without realizing it, we are ordering up more of the same for the future. It's like riding in the back seat of life, deferring to an automatic pilot that, without periodic reprogramming, will tend to drive in circles, repeating the behaviors of yesterday in the lock-step march Freud labeled our 'compulsion to repetition.'

If you're happy with the way your life has been going, then relax and enjoy the ride. But if you're tiring of the same old outcomes and the same old conversations, its time to vacate the back seat and regain control. That's what this weekend is all about. Helping you grab hold of the reins of your life and putting you back in the driver's seat."

The Moderator looks at his watch, then slowly scans the group. "The next hour has been reserved for 'unfinished business.' In a moment you'll decide whether the session has value for you or whether you'll use it as extra free time. It is now 3 PM. Whatever you decide, we'll all meet back here at 5 PM for our wrap-up session.

The 'unfinished business' hour is an ideal time to come face to face with an issue, a person or an event that continues to cause you confusion or upset. What you'll be doing is 'dialoguing' with an entity. It may be a person — perhaps your mother or father, your spouse or ex-spouse — a place, society in general, work, your body or even your Higher Power. The technique of journaling, of writing down your thoughts, is a proven method of getting at your deepest feelings, attitudes or fears and working them through. By so doing, we often tap into our unconscious and surface just what we need to see, hear, come to grips with and ultimately accept.

Let's take another five-minute stretch break in place. You can use the time to talk it over with your partner whether you wish or need to dialogue. Should you decide to stay, open your notebook to the dialogue tab when you're ready and simply follow the instructions."

Editor's Note: Proceed to page 199 if you have no unfinished business to resolve.

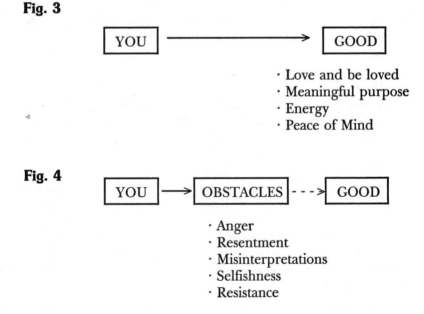

Fig. 3

YOU ⟶ GOOD

· Love and be loved
· Meaningful purpose
· Energy
· Peace of Mind

Fig. 4

YOU → OBSTACLES ⇢ GOOD

· Anger
· Resentment
· Misinterpretations
· Selfishness
· Resistance

Fig. 5

· Positive attitudes & beliefs
· Positive self-esteem
· Positive self-direction

Fig. 6

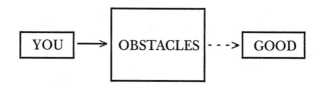

Fig. 7

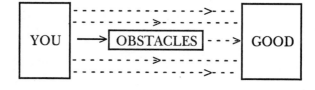

NOTES:
[1]Paul Kurtz, *Exuberance - A Philosophy of Happiness*, (Buffalo: Prometheus Books, 1977), p. 172.
[2]M. Scott Peck, *The Road Less Traveled*, (New York: Simon & Schuster, 1978), p. 230.

Chapter 9

UNFINISHED BUSINESS
(Optional)

You and your young Guide have decided to go to work on some important unfinished business. Per the Moderator's instruction, you open your notebook to the dialogue tab and pick up your pencil. The format is self-explanatory and you begin:

<u>Dialogue #1</u>

We would like to have a talk with _____.

Right now our relationship with that person or entity can best be described as _____ _____.

Milestone events in that relationship (list key persons, events or involvements):

- ◆ _____
- ◆ _____
- ◆ _____
- ◆ _____
- ◆ _____

Now begin your dialogue by making statements and letting the other respond. Continue a series of exchanges until the matter resolves itself.

After due reflection, you begin.

You: _____

_____

_____

Response: _____

_____

_____

You: _____

_____

_____

Response: _____

_____

_____

You: _____

_____

_____

Response: _____

_____

_____

You: _____

_____

_____

Response: _____

_____

_____

<u>Dialogue #2</u>

We would also like to have a talk with _____.

Right now our relationship with that person or entity can best be described as _____

Milestone events in that relationship (list key persons, events or involvements):

◆ _____

◆ _____

◆ _____

◆ _____

Now begin your dialogue by making statements and letting the other respond.

You: _____

_____

Response: _____

_____

You: _____

_____

Response: _____

_____

You: _____

_____

Response: _____

_____

◆ ◆ ◆
Free Time - 4-5 PM
◆ ◆ ◆

Chapter 10

WRAP UP — DAY ONE

It's a few minutes before 5 PM and the warmth of the receding sun is still a comfort. The Moderator is mingling with the early arrivals, unable to contain his passion for the subject matter. His enthusiasm for the weekend's process is palpably present in all that he does.

There's a quality about him you can't quite pinpoint. Moments earlier you experienced his charm and manner on a very personal level. During a brief chat he seemed to have the capacity to see you and your eight-year-old sidekick within the same singular glance; a glance that seemed to say "I understand where you've been and where you're going, and I'm behind you both 100%."

You watch as he makes his way back to the podium. You note the determined yet sincere manner in which he makes everyone feel somehow special. You hope one day to be similarly gifted and centered.

The large pad proclaims the theme for this final session. It contains but one word — MEANING. The Moderator is subdued as he begins. "You've come a long way in the last two days, but in actuality you've been partners a lot longer than that.

We all hunger for a meaning or a purpose in our lives. Often we can be misled to search for it, believing that it resides perhaps just around the next bend. We yield ever so slowly to the realization that the meaning we seek can only be found deep within ourselves; that we build meaning into our own lives — it's a gift we give ourselves — and we do it through our commitments.

Earlier in the weekend, you were asked to reflect on your commitments. There was no pressure at the time to identify what they were or if, in fact, you had made any. The focus was on explaining that dimension of maturity whereby we learn to live by meaning and by values which we choose, and that in order to avoid rocking-chair jobs and involvements, we need to 'listen in' to our own applause meter, to make choices based on our own needle readings, not on someone else's.

You spent the last two days getting back in touch with yourself. The emphasis has been on self-discovery and self-direction. Why? For the reason given by Theodore Reik, a contemporary of Sigmund Freud, who once said, 'Nothing said to us, nothing we can learn from others reaches so deep as that which we find in ourselves.'

Your young Guide has helped you explore yourself in ways you'll probably never be able to adequately express. And, in case you hadn't noticed, no thanks are necessary. To a child, they are absolutely delighted with who they will become. Their love for you is unbounded. Call it self-love if you like, I prefer to call it self-esteem. Its value transcends any monetary measurement. Perhaps your Guide will let you borrow some before you leave."

As the Moderator pauses, you jostle your young Guide's hair and kid about your mutual good taste. As your eyes meet, a private, shared smile quickly fills your heart to overflowing. You're not looking forward to saying goodbye in the morning. You resolve to savor your remaining time together and to cross that bridge when you come to it.

CLOSURE

Word had spread that the balance of the day after the 5 PM wrap up would be free time. You and your sidekick have planned something special, but before you'll let your thoughts jump ahead you're looking forward to drawing some conclusions.

Your wait is a short one. The Moderator pulls from his pocket some frayed, rabbit-eared index cards and begins, "Much of what I am I owe to the very experience you are completing today and to these cards. They guide me when I lose my way and sustain me when my spirit becomes troubled. They are a summary of what I learned when I sat where you do now many years ago.

They are a summary of what I've deeply desired to become and of the beliefs and attitudes I've wanted to have guide my thoughts and actions along the way. I have read them daily ever since. In the process, I so etched these thought pathways in my mind they gradually emerged on their own. I soon became that person and embodied those beliefs. I got back in touch with my own inner rhythm and brought the rest of my life into step. I became the person I was created to become.

It hasn't and it won't always be easy, but between these cards, your Higher Power and a special gift to come, you too can transform your life into the great adventure it was meant to be."

Even the youngsters are spellbound. Upon instruction, you open the notebook to the designated section. What you see are the contents of those rabbit-eared cards. The Moderator has chosen to share these personal statements to help you to fashion your own. You read through them carefully:

MY "BE-ATTITUDES"

To work and practice each day to be ...
...A good friend & father to my boys
...A good listener...and to meet!
...Faithful to me and to my own needle readings
...Creatively alive in the moment
...Dedicated to the truth and to undoing the
    tyranny of preconception
...A Star Thrower...to look for the good

MY GOALS

Overall....   to gather the collective wisdom of past and present thinkers for the overall purpose of enriching lives.

Family.....   to build self-esteem daily in my three sons

Career.....   to invest myself daily in M.E. Weekend activities.

Mental.....   to reaffirm my own self-esteem through daily practice of the cards and the one-minute pep talk.

Physical...   to avoid food and drink that impairs my thoughts and moods, and to maintain three times/week exercise program.

Social.....   to re-establish and tighten old friendships and be open for new ones...to practice "meeting" daily.

Community..to help others encountering difficulties along the way.

Spiritual...   to integrate my Higher Power into all of the above.

MY BELIEFS

I believe.......in me!

...in what I am in the process of becoming.

...in my own worth and goodness.

...in my three boys.

...that God is in my corner.

...in the power of a smile and a hug.

...in looking for the GOOD.

...in second chances.

...in living with passion and commitment.

...in living in the present and emphasizing listening.

...in love and compassion.

...in self-actualization.

...in the M.E. Weekend.

I AM IN THE PROCESS OF BECOMING.....

...a thoughtful father
...a published author
...an effective public speaker
...a self-actualization advocate
...a catalyst for "meeting" - first
myself...then others
...synonymous with the M.E. Weekend

THEREFORE, REMEMBER TO....

...Listen <u>IN</u>!
...Act on my needle readings
...Get my heart into it and <u>COMMIT</u>
...Read and practice these cards and the
one-minute pep talk daily
...Look for the GOOD in others and
in the moment
...Emphasize loving, not being loved
...Listen to others...and to <u>MEET</u>
...Hug my young Guide <u>often</u>

The Moderator seems almost apologetic about the ambitious nature of his career goals but reminds the group the intent of the cards is to capture and record what's in their hearts. "This is not an exercise to impress, but to focus and to remind. If you remember but one thing, remember this: you and only you can judge the value of an experience, a career or a goal for you...and you do it by listening in.

Please take your time. You may wish to review what you've written to date as a primer. To help you concentrate, the youngsters will be excused and treated to a movie across the street. Since having a central record of your weekend will be important later, complete the summary listings first in your notebook, then transfer them to cards when you return home. You'll also want to read the contents of the envelope the ushers are now passing out at that time."

As the envelopes are distributed and as the youngsters await to depart, the Moderator lovingly scans the group. He seems to be pausing to savor the mood, sharing in each awakening and renewal — capturing in his memory for lesser days to come the joy of this moment...of special people preparing for a new beginning, for a new standard of stewardship in their lives.

Beaming from head to toe, he thrusts his clasped hands once again above his head, sharing in the breakthroughs and basking in the glow of the love and newfound unity that abounds.

Before he releases the children, he asks the group to bow their heads and to give thanks to their Higher Power for the grace that has been bestowed upon them. As if on cue, the group instinctively links hands and pauses to give thanks in silence.

In the midst of the silence, your thoughts of thanks are interrupted by this powerful and unexpected display of group unity. It's as if the energy of the joined hands is passing through your arms and into your heart. You contemplate the shared struggle and realize you are not alone in this journey. These fellow travelers represent but a small fraction of a much broader fellowship. You give thanks for this additional moment of grace.

You're still deep in thought when the movie title is announced. The spontaneous cheer from the youngsters is reminiscent of that electric moment during a graduation ceremony when the final bell rings.

You hug your young partner and promise to work hard for the team on the final assignment. As quiet returns, you quickly occupy yourself with the task at hand. There is so much that has happened and that you want to remember. You pick up the pencil and begin:

MY GOALS

Overall..... _____

Family...... _____

Career...... _____

Mental...... _____

Physical.... _____

Social...... _____

Community.._____

Spiritual... _____

MY "BE-ATTITUDES"

To work and practice each day to.....

... _____

... _____

... _____

... _____

... _____

... _____

MY BELIEFS

I believe.......

... _____
... _____
... _____
... _____
... _____
... _____
... _____
... _____
... _____
... _____

I AM IN THE PROCESS OF BECOMING.....

... _____
... _____
... _____
... _____
... _____
... _____

THEREFORE, I MUST REMEMBER TO.....

... _____
... _____
... _____
... _____
... _____
... _____

The notebook has one last assignment that is presented as optional. You are instructed to return to page 138 to read your Epitaph. In the event your weekend experience has prompted you to amend what you've written, space is provided to do so now.

Revised Epitaph for _____ : _____

_____
_____
_____
_____

◆ ◆ ◆

Free time - Balance of the day

―――――――――――Chapter 11―――――――――――

THE LETTER

Dawn — Final Day

You awaken to the sounds of morning. Lying quietly, you delight to the background music of chirping birds. You're pleased with yourself for taking notice. You reflect back on the prior evening and your multiple attempts to express all you've come to feel for that precious little person in the next room. You peer through the door and drink in the vision of peaceful slumber. Your eyes mist over as you recall the tender moments you've shared and you search for some final farewell gesture that can capture your intense feelings.

You decide to write your young soul mate a letter — a very special letter, straight from your heart, that will place loving salve exactly where you and only you could know it's needed. You see the letter as a way to reach around the years and extend a parental embrace that those beautiful little hands can turn to whenever the path becomes bumpy or the spirit needs nourishment. If you must say goodbye, the letter will permit you to give portability to these feelings and to be there in spirit whenever you're needed.

Your sadness over the pending farewell is allayed as you focus on writing this most important of all letters.

Dear _____,

_____

_____

_____

_____

_____

_____

_____

_____

_____

_____

_____

_____

_____

_____

_____

_____

_____

_____

_____

_____

_____

_____

_____

_____

_____

_____

_____

_____

_____

◆ ◆ ◆

Chapter 12

THE GIFT

Departure

Breakfast flies by in a whirl of remembrances and loving reassurance. Before you know it, the morning has passed and you're hand-and-hand headed for the edge of town. In spite of the emotion of the moment, you manage to miss all the sidewalk cracks. This is one part of the weekend you hope will soon fade, but you nonetheless are happy with your performance.

As the perimeter of the Neighborhood approaches, the ground fog that had shrouded the area upon your arrival seems to have returned. While your mind is searching for just the right words of farewell, you enter the edge of the fog. You recall the cleansing effect of a few days prior but the sensation is altogether different today. It's as if time is slowing down. You have a sense you're both moving in slow motion and there's a strange energy emanating from your joined hands. Before either of you can comment, you embrace one last time. You find yourself wishing the embrace could last forever.

As you cling together in the fog, the mysterious energy spreads from your hands and envelops you both. In a delirious and magical moment, you feel yourself floating, actually taken up and somehow turned inside out and then back again. In the process, you and your young Guide have become one.

You pause in disbelief as you attempt to comprehend what has just occurred. Your mind flashes back to the Moderator's opening comments, something about a farewell gift that would assist you when your journey through life resumed.

The magnitude and profoundness of this gift renders you speechless. You're aware of a new duality — a new integrated outlook — in your thoughts and in your manner. You embrace the vividness of your new inner child, thinking of all the adventures you will now share together. You reflect on the strength of this new partnership. You feel bolstered by the infusion of the self-esteem your young Guide so genuinely felt for you, and you are warmed by the thought of that final letter, and being present now to ensure its uplifting message reaches your inner child whenever the need arises.

As you collect your thoughts, you are rejoined by your earlier escort. If it weren't for the notebook and envelope in your hand, you might think you had just returned from an extended and elaborate daydream. As you relate the highlights of your M.E. Weekend, you're aware of an inner peace and a calmness both in yourself and in your escort. You pause to hug your inner child and to marvel at your new, balanced perspective. You're filled with warmth and hopeful expectation of the things you and your inner child will now accomplish together.

The walk home should be a delight, and best of all, its only just the beginning.

Section 2

RETURNING HOME

Chapter 13

CONTINUED A.C.C.E.S.S.

There's something different about your escort. Something that you can't quite place. In the course of relating your M.E. Weekend experience, you realize it is not your escort who has changed, but that perhaps you have.

As you marvel at your enhanced ability to listen and to perceive — what Martin Buber described as "meeting" — you take a moment to celebrate this early dividend with you inner child. You celebrate with a hug.

The celebration is not lost on your escort who, as you look up, has already joined in. Incredibly, he raises his clasped hands and shakes them above his head, then with a knowing smile pats you on the shoulder.

He explains, "The heightened presence of your inner child within you is the greatest of all possible gifts. As you've just seen and demonstrated, the ability to stop and savor the moment is a wonderful skill; a skill you and your inner child can now develop together. In fact, you're already well on your way.

While we're on the subject of stopping — and since you seem to enjoy hugging your inner child — there's a marvelous practice you might wish to consider. In his book *One Minute For Myself*, Dr. Spencer Johnson suggests 'only when you stop doing what doesn't work can things get better.'[1]   He goes on to describe how many of us get focused on 'being loved' rather than on 'loving.'

If we don't feel loved we tend to withdraw and in the process fail to act in a loving way, thereby making it more difficult for others to love us. We compromise our important relationships, fail to nurture our loved ones and end up precluding and blocking the very thing we most desire.

The good news is your inner child can help you avoid this trap in the future. As Dr. Johnson suggests, when things aren't going well and you're about to respond badly, stop and ask yourself, 'Is there a better way right now for me to take good care of me'[2] ...a better way to take good care of my inner child?"

Your escort has grown animated and his enthusiasm is real. You give him your full attention.

He continues, "The secret is to derail any culprit automatic thoughts before negative feelings get triggered and before your behavior goes south. Your inner child can play a key new role in this offensive. What you're trying to do is break the tension and that negative thought cycle by substituting a replacement thought which in this case will be a replacement image. Instead of allowing the negative flow to play out, override it by picturing your inner child...then pause for a hug.

With that image firmly fixed in your mind, ask yourself, 'Is there a better way right now for me to take good care of my inner child?' You'll no doubt find you'll hug your way into a much better place and your response will likely be 180 degrees away from where you might otherwise end up."

You feel particularly close to your inner child at the moment and are more than willing to give it a try. The idea of being able to catch yourself is attractive. Your instincts, however, must be honored and you find yourself questioning and wondering if you'll remember to remember. Your escort shares the concern and offers the following suggestion.

"The intense experience you've just concluded gives you a tremendous advantage in being able to quickly and effortlessly picture your young Guide. I purposely use the word 'guide' because that's who will guide you through this and supply the inspiration.

One of the secrets to making it work is provided in Dr. Johnson's book. Rather than getting angry and criticizing another, Dr. Johnson suggests we disrupt that flow and insert the following replacement thought: 'They are doing the best they can right now.'

In other words, once you've taken the proverbial deep breath, take it one step further and look beneath the troublesome behavior to observe the Child or Parent tape that is causing him or her trouble; the Child or Parent whose dominant tape continues to get air time. When viewed in the context of these inner pulls, the thought — 'they are doing the best they can right now' — will be much easier to entertain and sustain."

You walk along in silence, each contemplating the powerful experience which continues to unfold. You recall your escort's earlier claim that the experience you were setting out on was one of self-discovery and self-renewal. He has proven to be a man of his word.

You have a much clearer sense of who you are and what you want to accomplish. You've also acquired — or been reunited with — an old companion who, unlike all others, can steadfastly keep you pointed, on track and in touch with that most important of all applause meters...your own; that applause meter whose needle readings are becoming more and more audible to you as you remember to 'listen in.' Your inner Guide is seeing to it.

Your escort is particularly ebullient as he describes where all this is leading.

"When the emotional tide has turned; when your thoughts, feelings and actions are in congruence; when your self-initiated activity leads to evident results and achievements, energy is released. The process is reinforced, repeated, reinforced, etc., until a new habitual way of thinking and acting is established."

Speaking with the conviction of someone who has lived the program himself, he continues, "At some point, your dedication to reviewing and practicing your index cards and the new mental pathways thus created will enable your conscious mind to relax and your subconscious to take over. When that happens, you're said to be 'in the zone.'"

IN THE ZONE

Your escort explains that the expression "in the zone" is borrowed from the world of sports. Various professional athletes over time have described a level of performance that has an almost mystical quality; they have a sense of "knowing" just before something happens, time seems to slow down, and their performance seems effortless. Investigations into the phenomenon have tended to find the common denominator to be a conscious mind that has been quieted. Athletes who have trained their bodies and minds, so when called upon to perform, they quiet the chatter in their minds, freeing themselves from any mental or emotional distraction.

New research into the brain has monitored an interesting relationship between skill level and brain activity. Surprisingly, as the subject's skill level increased, the metabolic rate of the brain slowed down. Consistent with this have been findings that higher levels of metabolism correlate with worse performance. The one exception to this has been in the visual cortex — the part of the brain that processes visual imagery. Here the metabolic rate increases with skill development, suggesting that the subject is able to process more visual information as his or her skill increases.

The connection escapes you until your escort explains, "The reason I bring this up is simply this. Our ability to listen and to be centered in the moment is a function of computer time or available mental processing capacity. If our minds are invested in rehashing the past or worrying about the future, or erecting defense mechanisms because we are not in congruence, the chatter level in our consciousness will impair the ability of our visual cortex to process incoming visual information.

If our purpose in life is to 'meet' and if we meet through listening, then we want to devote our full consciousness to the task. To the extent we can chart a course for ourselves that is in step with our inner rhythm — with our motivational pattern — we'll find that our thoughts, feelings and actions begin to converge. Gradually, we'll be in a better position to quiet our conscious mind and allow ourselves to gain access to an ancient wiring system that expands our capacity to process visual information, enhancing our ability to listen and take on input, often slowing time in the process, and releasing a form of euphoric energy. This energy is born from accomplishment and from the growing realization we can re-create our lives.

One does not need to be a professional athlete to avail himself or herself of these benefits. Once sampled, the practitioner will gladly embrace a regimen that promises 'continued access' to the zone — access to the balanced calmness that is endemic there and to the energy and mood-enhancing feelings triggered when we find ourselves making headway on an important goal, a frequent occurrence when in the zone."

You question whether being in the zone and being in congruence are one and the same. Your escort responds, "Absolutely, and as we've been reviewing, you get there by identifying your motivational pattern and committing to a direction that leverages that pattern and facilitates your becoming the person you were created to be. This direction respects your inborn preferences and rhythms and brings the rest of your life into conformity.

Between the index cards you'll be creating when you arrive home and your most precious of all gifts — conscious possession of your inner child — you're a natural to succeed. The pieces are all in place."

As your escort pauses to collect his thoughts, you become aware of how much he resembles your weekend Moderator. You're surprised you hadn't noticed it sooner. Exhibiting the same passion for the subject, he continues, "You're almost home. Perhaps only inches away from tapping into your own energy geyser, or maybe it's already begun. The fact that you're here shows you've decided to take control.

Let's review what we know about you. Your desire to improve is real. Your very presence on this 'walk' suggests you accept responsibility for your life and for your own happiness and peace of mind. The time and effort put into your M.E. Weekend experience has strengthened your sense of direction and purpose. Now you're going to return home and cement your new commitment by transferring your thoughts to index cards and beginning a twenty-one day entry or transition investment. During this time, your daily efforts at practicing and visualizing the contents of your cards will begin to etch the necessary new pathways in your mind and consciousness. In time your thoughts will naturally gravitate there and you will begin to embody and become the person you were meant to be."

You're elated with your weekend experience and with what you've gleaned from the walk to this point. You find your thoughts racing ahead to what awaits as you implement and put into practice all that you've learned. The presence of your Guide within you is a particular joy and reason enough for celebration.

Before you can begin to express your gratitude, your escort directs your attention to your notebook, or rather to the envelope you received the prior evening. At his suggestion, you sit down on a nearby knoll to inspect its contents. As you remove the enclosed document, your escort recounts his earlier comments about how one might gain "continued access" to the zone. Somehow you're not surprised to find the envelope contains a compendium of just such tips, expressed in a way to help you catalogue them for each retrieval. The title of the document provokes a smile from both of you. It reads:

❖ ❖ ❖

CONTINUED *A*.C.C.E.S.S.
Anger

On the subject of anger, we can be brief...remove it. If you're still in touch with anger and with blaming, you're likely not solving. Remember your inner child. The next time you feel compelled to react angrily or to criticize another, remember the tension breaker we discussed. Pause for a moment to embrace your inner child, then say to yourself "they are doing the best they can right now."

The same goes for how you handle yourself. A good exercise is to listen to the way you speak to yourself when you make a mistake. If you tend to beat yourself up, use the same tension breaker. Picture your inner child, pause for a hug, then ask if there's a better way for you to take good care of yourself...to take good care of your inner child.

Anger is terribly destructive and often exacts its greatest toll on the person wielding it...on the person harboring the resentment and fury. You can't go the distance with too much resistance, and anger, an emotional prison of the worst kind that will block your growth and happiness for as long as you continue to give it life and air time.

❖ ❖ ❖

Continued A.*C*.C.E.S.S.
Communication

One way to ensure that anger doesn't get a foothold in your life is to have a well-developed communications network functioning as a stress release valve.

With anger often resulting from unexpressed feelings and unmet needs, our interpersonal relationships are where we most need to look for the GOOD. Unfortunately, in our rush to interpret the intent or meaning of what another says or does, we often fail to listen to the feelings being communicated beneath the words or actions...the feelings being pushed to the surface perhaps by their Child or Parent memory bank. In our rush to interpret, we frequently misinterpret. To the extent you can continue to consciously possess your inner child, your self-esteem will be enhanced and all your relationships will benefit from your heightened abilities to listen — to be alert for the inner child in others — and to forgive.

While we're on the subject of communication, have you ever noticed how boaters, runners, skiers, etc., wave to one another? It's a friendly gesture that simply recognizes a shared interest. For that very reason, we should smile and acknowledge the presence of strangers within close proximity to ourselves simply because we share a far more intimate and personal interest — to love and be loved — and because we recognize each opportunity, albeit brief, to support the struggle of others and to be an agent of peace, understanding and acceptance and to be a Star Thrower, focused on celebrating the small moments of life. Having grasped the reality that life's gifts are fleeting and that we are often heedless of them, we choose to remember, from Thornton Wilder's *Our Town*, little Emily's impassioned plea, "Mamma, Poppa, let's look at one another while yet we may."

In the world of relationships, share the gift of your best self — your new, integrated self — with you first and then with others. Peace is both the absence of anger and the presence of love, beginning with love for yourself. Your young Guide has enough for both of you. Stay close.

❖ ❖ ❖

Continued A.C.*C*.E.S.S.
Commitment

Many of us go in search of meaning and purpose, hoping to find it perhaps around the next bend. We yield ever so slowly to the realization that meaning and happiness can only be found internally, not externally. They are gifts we give ourselves and we acquire them through our commitments.

Robert Bly is an American poet who Bill Moyers has labeled a modern day troubadour. He employs myth and lyrical fairy tales to register his sharp insights. On this subject of purpose, Bly spins a tale about a conversation that takes place between a man and the wind. It seems the odor of jasmine is in the air and the man wishes to bring it forth. The wind offers to exchange it for the odor of the man's roses. Regrettably, the man reports his flowers are all dead. Upon hearing this, the wind inquires "What have you done with the garden entrusted to you?"[3]

The same penetrating question has triggered many a midlife crisis, "What have you done — what are you doing— with your life?" With many of us taking the gift of time for granted, squandering it on inconsequential pursuits — reacting and not initiating — is it any wonder chronic depression, substance abuse and apathy in schools, in relationships and in the work place are so prevalent. We have to finally answer — to no one's satisfaction but our own — what have we committed ourselves to? What have we planted in our garden?

Continued A.C.C.*E*.S.S.
Encouragement

What Martin Buber, the late Jewish philosopher, meant by his injunction to "confirm the other" in our relationships was nothing more than good, old-fashioned encouragement. To recognize, in others and in ourselves, that we are never "done deals," that life is an organic process filled with new beginnings and a relentless flowing on, and that just as we need periodic encouragement to keep our own journey and struggle buoyant, so too do others.

As we learn to draw strength and encouragement from the presence of our inner child, we should encourage others to do likewise. By gradually embodying the qualities we aspire to, our whole demeanor will serve as a billboard for emulation. Because of its reverberative effect, as we treat ourselves and others with compassion and understanding, we'll experience the truth of the adage "what goes around comes around." We eventually get what we give...love and understanding.

❖ ❖ ❖

Continued A.C.C.E.*S*.S.
Striving

In his book *Exuberance - A Philosophy of Happiness*, Paul Kurtz insightfully observed: "It is in the process of attainment that we thrive."[4] David Viscott said it equally well when he wrote in his book *Risking*: "The worth of your efforts to you is not that they are great, but that they are yours...that you tried, that you gave your life a meaning from which you could take strength, making you feel whole."[5] Only by risking to give your dream life and form can you break free from the past and center yourself in the moment. Only then will you book passage through Martin Luther's Red Sea, free to become the best that you can be.

The action begins in your heart. Listen in for your inner rhythm, then commit to pursuing a direction that stirs a passion, that moves you out into the main current of your life's flow. Only then will your life take on a semblance of the great adventure Helen Keller described. Only then will you experience an inner sense of peace, as the person you are converges with the person you were created to be, inch-by-inch becoming less a slave to your early conditioning and more and more a person who lives by choice and self-direction.

❖ ❖ ❖

Continued A.C.C.E.S.S.
Solitude

Build some solitude into your routine — time set aside once or twice a week, where you can get away and do something just for you. Make time to take a walk, read a book, or spend your coffee break or lunch hour alone; time to let your thoughts decant and for your perspective and priorities to reset and sort themselves out.

Don't expect others to schedule this time for you. This is your job and your responsibility. As that sneaker commercial exhorts, "Just Do It!" Besides, we're betting your young Guide will step forward if you need any reminders.

You're a team now and what a marvelous team at that. Imagine the possibilities of being able to spend each and every day with someone you know, love and respect; someone you can always trust to be there and who thinks the world of you and always will. A friend like that deserves a hug...lots of them.

No thanks are necessary. Just pass it on as best you can.

NOTES:
[1] Dr. Spencer Johnson, *One Minute For Myself*, (New York: William Morrow & Co., 1985), p. 94.
[2] Ibid. p. 19.
[3] Robert Bly, *A Gathering of Men*, PBS Telecast, 1989.
[4] Paul Kurtz, *Exuberance - A Philosophy of Happiness*, (Buffalo: Prometheus Books, 1977), p. 175.
[5] Dr. David Viscott, *Risking*, (New York: Simon & Schuster, 1977), p. 208.

EPILOGUE

The walk has proven to be a cornucopia of remembrances and insights. You fumble for words of thanks, settling for a warm handshake and an unrestrained smile. There's a strange new duality to your smile. You both pause to honor it.

His mission almost complete, your escort continues: "As we grow in love and acceptance of ourselves, the echoes from our past subside, releasing us to meet and embrace the GOOD around us. We are free to become creatively alive in the moment and free to meet others now that we have finally met ourselves. Free to understand what Martin Buber intuited long ago that 'the kingdom is buried in our midst — between us.'[1]

As Walter Truett Anderson observed in his book *The Upstart Spring*: 'Perhaps there is something political in the human potential movement. Perhaps the humane society the civil rights activists and peace protesters seek is to be reached by a long march through the psyche, through countless acts of personal transformation.'[2] Perhaps in a world increasingly alarmed by environmental pollution, we need to spend equal time turning inward and addressing the internal pollution that might be continuing to contaminate our thoughts, our feelings and — most importantly — our self-image. By changing how we experience ourselves we change the central program that drives all our perceptions and interpretations. We change how we see and relate to the world and how the world in turn relates to us.

Richard Louv, the award-winning journalist and author of *America II*, sees a road in America's future leading to a new potential...'where there is an intensified sense of responsibility and the realization that the farther society disperses physically, the more we need human connections...that down this road we'll form stronger and more lasting bonds of family and friendship; instead of walled enclaves, neighborhoods that will reach out. At these destinations, which are not so much out there as they are within ourselves, we could find our place and touch each other. Down that road lies home.' "[3]

◆ ◆ ◆

As Martin Luther is purported to have observed from his work on the Bible, "What else is our time on earth than a personal passage through the Red Sea." It is a journey where we strive to break free from the bondage of the human condition.

Your M.E. Weekend experience has been structured to be a catalyst for that breaking-free process; a jump-start push along the road to regaining control of the balance of your life...toward greater fulfillment and peace of mind. With your car now in sight, you ask your escort if he has any concluding advice. As if reminded by the request, he raises his eyebrows and in a calm, fatherly manner advises, "Give yourself permission to try, permission to fail and plenty of hugs along the way.

Now that you've been reunited with your inner child, all the pieces are at hand. The stage is set...the rest is up to you. It's time to 'take away the stone' and let the sun back into your life. It's time to live like you really mean it and get your heart into it. It's time to look for the GOOD along the way and to be a Star Thrower...to invest in life, starting with your own.

Martin Buber had a viewpoint that I'd like to leave you with. He felt strongly that God speaks to us through daily events. 'Happening upon happening, situation upon situation, are enabled and empowered by the personal speech of God to demand of the human person that he take his stand and make his decision.'[4]

It's time to take *your* stand.

It's time.

Your inner Guide will help you every step of the way. Be mindful of St. Thomas Aquinas' instruction that happiness is the conscious possession of a good. Now that you're in conscious possession of your inner child, the final puzzle piece is in place. You're ready to embark on the most rewarding and most adventurous chapter in your life...the one that starts today.

Your future is not in the stars, but it is in the cards...the cards you're now going to write up and practice everyday. Don't commit to try it. Commit to do it.

Remember, give yourself permission to try, permission to fail and plenty of hugs along the way.

Good luck, God speed...and pass it on."

NOTES:
[1] Martin Buber, *I and Thou*, (New York: Charles Scribner's Sons, 1958), p. 120.
[2] Walter Truett Anderson, *The Upstart Spring*, (Menlo Park, Ca.: Addison-Wesley, 1983), p. 291.
[3] Richard Louv, *America II*, (Los Angeles: J.P. Tarcher, 1983), p. 257.
[4] Buber, pp. 136-137.